Preparing the Nation's Teachers to Teach Reading:

A Manifesto in Defense of "Teacher Educators
Like Me"

Preparing the Nation's Teachers to Teach Reading

A Manifesto in Defense of "Teacher Educators Like Me"

Curt Dudley-Marling

GARN PRESS

NEW YORK, NY

Published by Garn Press, LLC
New York, NY
www.garnpress.com

Book and cover design by Benjamin J. Taylor
Cover image by Benjamin J. Taylor

Library of Congress Control Number: 2015945780

Publisher's Cataloging-in-Publication Data

Dudley-Marling, Curt.
    Preparing the nation's teachers to teach reading : a manifesto in defense of "teacher educators like me" / Curt Dudley-Marling.
        pages cm
    Includes bibliographical references.
    ISBN: 978-1-942146-20-9 (pbk.)
    ISBN: 978-1-942146-21-6 (e-book)
    1. Teachers—Training of—United States. 2. Teachers—Rating of—United States. 3. Teacher educators—United States. 4. Public schools—United States. 5. Privatization in education—United States.
    6. Propaganda, Capitalist—United States.   I. Title.
LB1715 .D83 2015
370.71`173 —dc23
                    2015945780

Not long after I began this book I formally retired from Boston College. I now spend my days biking, playing the guitar, walking the dogs, reading and traveling with my wife, Chris. The drumbeat of criticism of schools and teachers no longer affects me as it once did. I am mindful, however, that the nation's teachers continue to struggle daily with the burdens of withering criticisms of their work, budget cuts, attacks on tenure and other benefits, competition from alternative programs that threaten job security and on and on. This is in addition to the fact that teachers work incredibly hard to do their jobs effectively. So it is to the nation's teachers that I dedicate this book. We are all grateful for your hard work and dedication. You are one of our country's greatest resources.

Contents

Foreword by Marilyn Cochran-Smith   1

Introduction   9

Are Professors Like Me Ruining Our Schools?   11

The National Council on Teacher Quality   14

NCTQ 2.0   17

NCTQ 3.0   23

Why Reading Educators Like Me Resist NCTQ's Idea of "Scientifically Based Research"   27

Reading educators like me: "The reason children in American schools are failing to keep up ..."   29

What Reading Educators Like Me Believe and Do Not Believe About Reading – And Why   35

A Sociocultural Theory of Reading   40

A Meaning-based Perspective on the Teaching of Reading   50

Reading Educators as Producers of Knowledge   66

What NCTQ and Other Reform Groups Want/What Reading Educators Like Me Want   69

What Reformers Want   70

What Progressive Reading Educators Want   78

Notes   87

References   89

Appendix   97

About The Author Curt Dudley-Marling   103

Other Books By Curt Dudley-Marling   104

Foreword by Marilyn Cochran-Smith

This little book, which is titled a "manifesto" that defends teacher educators like him, was written by Curt Dudley-Marling, my periodic collaborator and co-author and my long-time colleague and friend. For nearly 20 years, Curt and I worked together at Boston College—as faculty members in the same department, readers of the same dissertations, steadfast supporters of the doctoral advisory committee, collaborating editors for a major teacher education journal, and—more times than we cared to count—not-so-patient co-attendees at long meetings that raised questions about what it really means to do good work in the world of teacher education research, policy and practice.

During those two decades, Curt and I often talked about emerging ideas, and we sometimes read each other's' partly-finished work, offering feedback, questions, and suggestions. But the joint professional activity we engaged in most frequently and the one that was by far, at least for me, the most valuable—was a kind of mutual reality checking about the rapidly changing educational policy scene, which grew increasingly more neo-liberal—and, as part of that, increasingly more publicized, politicized and contentious—over time.

In keeping with our long history, I regarded Curt's request that I write the Foreword to his book as a request for a reality check about the politics of education, particularly the politics of teacher education, which

1

has changed so dramatically since we began to work together as university professors 20 years ago, although we had known each prior to that time, and both of us already had two decades of experience in other universities before circumstances brought us together at Boston College. As his provocative title captures perfectly, Curt's manifesto focuses explicitly on the work of teacher educators who prepare teachers to teach children to read and to develop as life-time readers over time.

As I see it, Curt's book makes two important contributions. First, it carefully and rationally "defends" his lifetime's work, laying out with exquisite clarity and patience the major and inter-connected assumptions of a meaning-centered approach to teaching and learning reading. In the process of doing so, the book talks back in no uncertain terms to the excoriating critiques of meaning-centered reading teacher educators like Curt, critiques that are instantiated most visibly in multiple reports from the National Council on Teacher Quality (NCTQ) that allege the near total failure of university teacher educators to teach the nation's prospective teachers how to teach reading, thus presumably contributing to, if not causing, the alleged failure of many of the nation's children to learn to read well.

Although Curt himself describes his book as "polemical," I don't find it so. The book is outspoken and bold, to be sure, and the same critics who attacked the positions Curt attempted to explain in his posts on the Literacy Leaders listserv (described in his introduction to the book) will undoubtedly reject and attack his ideas here as well, if they ever have the occasion to read them. But polemics are often all ideology and no data, all passion and no reasoned principles of practice, all opposition and no proposition about alternative approaches and perspectives. Curt's book isn't like that at all. His propositions are grounded in a consistent, research-based, and principled theoretical framework for understanding the nature of teaching and learning to read, with many references to highly-regarded and well-vetted empirical research and to actual classroom experiences (his own and others') that support and helped to generate these propositions. His oppositions, especially to NCTQ's operating assumptions about reading, teaching reading, and preparing teachers to teach reading, are also grounded in carefully explained and principled theoretical frameworks, which are widely shared by literacy scholars and practitioners around the country and the world.

Curt's opposition to NCTQ's conclusions are further substantiated by his original – and I would say startling –analyses that show no correlation whatsoever between NCTQ's ratings of the approaches of the teacher education programs within a given state to preparing teachers to teach reading, on the one hand, and, on the other hand, the performance of the students in those states on NAEP reading tests, referred to as the nation's report card and widely regarded as the most valid national assessment of students' achievement.

The accuracy of Curt's conclusions about the lack of predictive validity of the NCTQ's ratings is supported by a new study that was released after he had completed the manuscript for this book. Using data from the state of North Carolina, Henry and Bastian (2015) found that in only one of 42 comparisons between graduates from programs with higher and lower NCTQ ratings did teachers from higher rated programs have higher value added scores, based on the achievement of their students. They concluded:

> "With our data and analyses, we do not find strong relationships between the performance of [teacher preparation program] graduates and NCTQ's overall program ratings or meeting NCTQ's standards" (p. 1).[1]

Curt's findings, along with Henry and Bastian's evidence about the failure of NCTQ ratings to predict teacher effectiveness, are difficult to ignore or dismiss on empirical grounds. I suspect, however, that NCTQ spokespersons will respond to this evidence—if at all—on ideological and political, rather than empirical, grounds. This brings me to the second major contribution of this book.

Curt raises very important questions about whether NCTQ's critiques of reading teacher education (and teacher education more broadly) can in any way at all be considered a good faith effort to make US teacher education better, as NCTQ claims its purpose is, or whether their critiques are a thinly-veiled contribution to the larger neoliberal agenda whose ultimate purpose is to undermine public education and university teacher education. The neoliberal education reform project that is intended to reinvent American education (and teacher education) is based on a completely economic conceptualization, which sets directions and limits for public policy and defines many education policy debates in terms of means, not ends. As Curt points out, a problematic aspect of the neoliberal education reform agenda is that the ultimate freedom is taken to be the freedom of the market. At the same time, from a neoliberal perspective, private goods and individual choices are more important than protecting and advancing the collective good, which is a fundamental precept of a democratic society.

From the very beginning of its project to review teacher preparation programs in the US and consistently all along the way, NCTQ has claimed—and on the surface at least, apparently without irony—to be a friend of teacher education, intent on earnest, constructive critique that can protect consumers, improve teacher preparation, and hold programs accountable for outcomes. But, as is widely known in the teacher education community, because of resistance by universities to provide information to NCTQ, some evidence was obtained by paying students for course syllabi or through federal Freedom of Information Act petitions. These covert actions are difficult to understand as research methods and data collection strategies unless they are politically motivated.

Moreover, as Curt points out, although NCTQ claims that its 19 standards and indicators were the result of years of research and expert analysis, the standards were never vetted by the professional community, nor were NCTQ's previous studies subjected to peer review. In addition, the current NCTQ advisory board includes Michael Barber, the chief education advisor of Pearson, Inc., Joel Klein, E.D. Hirsch, Chester Finn, Wendy Kopp, Eric Hanushek, and Rick Hess, a veritable who's who of the conservative opposition to university teacher education, long interested in breaking up its "monopoly" through deregulation and letting the market decide who gets fully prepared and fully certified teachers. These and many of the other "facts" about NCTQ revealed in Curt's book cast serious doubts about NCTQ's self-proclaimed larger purpose and raise difficult questions about whose interests are actually served by NCTQ's calculating and publically disseminating program ratings.

A partial answer to these questions may come in the form of knowledge about ERAOs, or "Education Reform Advocacy Organizations," which have emerged as powerful new policy players as one part of the post-*No Child Left Behind* (NCLB) politics of education (McGuinn, 2012b). ERAOs share funding sources, such as the Gates, Broad and Walton Family Foundations, and they also share reform ideologies aligned with neo-liberal approaches to school reform and campaign tactics. The largest and most prominent ERAOs are arguably StudentsFirst, founded and, until relatively recently, directed by Michelle Rhee, and Jeb Bush's Foundation for Excellence in Education. ERAOs formed a partnership in 2007 known as PIE, the Policy Innovators in Education Network, which currently supports 49 ERAOs in 31 states (McGuinn, 2012a). PIE's mission is to close the achievement gap, ensure that all students are college and career ready, replace low performing schools, protect charter schools and other choice options, and develop powerful accountability systems that link data on students, teachers, teacher preparation, school districts and states. To try to sort out what's really going on with the NCTQ teacher prep review, it helps to know that NCTQ is an ERAO and a partner in PIE. It's supported by the Gates, Broad and Walton Family Foundations, as well as the Fordham Foundation. Notwithstanding its own claims to the contrary, this information makes it very clear what NCTQ's larger agenda is.

NCTQ has been operating for more than 15 years now. During this time, there has been a major shift in the policy rhetoric about teacher quality in the U.S.—from a demand for "highly qualified teachers" to a demand for "highly effective teachers" (Hess & McShane, 2014). Consistent with this shift, today's most visible efforts to improve teacher education quality focus squarely on accountability, assuming that the major driver of education reform is accountability and evaluation. That is, they assume that the key to reform is assessing, rating and ranking states, institutions, programs, and teacher candidates, and they assume that rewards for the winners and consequences for the losers will bring about change. It is well worth looking closely at initiatives like NCTQ, as Curt has done in this book, in part because they are deeply revealing of the dominant values in our society. By specifying what teachers should know and be able to do, how they should be judged ready—or not—to teach, and how their preparation programs should be evaluated, initiatives like NCTQ's annual teacher prep review, with its explicit focus on how the nation's teachers are prepared to teach reading, reflect how those in power are seeking to shape the world for future citizens.

I regard this book as Curt's take on the current state of affairs in teacher education. I conclude my Foreword to the book—my reality check on Curt's perceptions—with good news and bad news. The good news is that I find his reading of the current situation accurate and insightful regarding both teacher preparation in general and the preparation of teachers to teach reading in particular. The bad news is that this means we are in a very problematic—even dangerous—situation. NCTQ's reviews of teacher preparation programs along with the positions of those who attacked Curt's listserv posts about meaning-centered reading are part of a larger social movement for "ed reform." This movement includes a number of other current accountability initiatives related to teacher education, such as the 2014 proposed federal reporting regulations for teacher preparation programs and states, which would be part of Title II of the Higher Education Act, as well as the standards of the newly-constituted Council for the Accreditation of Educator Preparation (CAEP), both of which will evaluate teacher preparation programs in part on the basis of the value their graduates add to students' growth and test scores.

The "ed reform" movement is based on the assumption that both education in general and teacher education in particular are the keys to the economic prosperity of the nation. But both of these systems are assumed to be "broken," and so they need to be fixed through the implementation of sophisticated new big-data systems that hold teachers, schools and teacher education programs accountable for students' achievement, as measured by tests. This approach has taken hold so extensively in the US that it is now broadly considered simply common sense.

Unfortunately, I believe that the initiatives of "ed reform," including the one described in Curt's book, may be collectively *de*forming rather than *re*forming teacher education by reshaping its goals and expectations in subtractive ways and redefining how teacher educators, like Curt and me and many of our colleagues around the country, understand our roles by giving us a singular and limited focus on test-based accountability. Slowly but surely, the ed reform movement is reducing the spaces in our work as teacher educators for discussion, action and advocacy related to equity and social justice (Cochran-Smith, 2014, 2015). Hopefully Curt's manifesto will be widely read and will contribute to a counter movement that challenges the assumptions, strategies and goals of "ed reform," and raises questions about who the winners and losers are when "ed reform" becomes common sense.

Marilyn Cochran-Smith
Boston College
May, 2015

Introduction

I wrote this brief text as a manifesto in defense of teacher educators like me, specifically, teacher educators who are in the business of preparing future teachers to teach reading. But it didn't start that way. When I began writing this little book, it was mainly going to center on a critique of the various reports written by the National Council of Teacher Quality (NCTQ) on teacher education in the United States, particularly NCTQ's conclusion that, overwhelmingly, prospective teachers in the US are not well prepared to teach early reading. In my opinion, the methodology of the NCTQ reports is fatally flawed and, therefore, the conclusions of the NCTQ report lack any validity whatsoever.

As a first step in examining the validity of the NCTQ reports, two of my Boston College colleagues (Marilyn Cochran-Smith and Larry Ludlow) and I looked at the relationship between NCTQ's assessment of how well teacher education programs in particular states are preparing teachers to teach early reading, and how well the students in those states actually perform in reading based on the most recent *National Assessment of Educational Progress* (NAEP) assessments of 4th grade reading performance. As I detail below, we found virtually no relationship between the NCTQ assessment of teacher education programs and reading achievement in particular states. Indeed, we found a slight negative correlation between the proportion of teacher education programs in individual states that met NCTQ's criteria for how well prepared teachers are to teach reading and 4th grade NAEP reading scores.

I began with the goal of building on this finding as part of a broader critique of NCTQ and its methods. But about the time I began writing this book I found myself under attack on a Literacy Leaders listserv after I posted a comment disputing how reading educators with whom I am associated (reading educators who take a meaning-based approach to the teaching of reading) were represented in a series of posts about reading instruction in the US. I will say more about this shortly. So what emerged was a text that includes a critique of NCTQ and the various reports it has issued as part of a broad defense of teacher educators, particularly teacher educators like me who are responsible for preparing prospective teachers to teach reading.

I begin this text by first sharing my experience on the literacy leaders listserv that led this text in a somewhat different direction from what I imagined. I then offer a pointed critique of the various reports NCTQ has issued on how well prospective teachers are prepared to teach reading. Next I respond to NCTQ's claims by outlining the theory and research that leads reading educators like me to reject the perspective on reading and reading instruction that is at the heart of both the NCTQ reports and most other critics of "meaning-based" approaches to reading instruction. In particular, I detail what reading educators like me believe about reading and reading instruction. Finally, I argue that the various NCTQ reports are part of a larger effort to discredit public schooling as a way of paving the way for market-based alternatives to traditional public schools. Like any good manifesto this text is deliberately polemical, although I make every effort to draw on substantial theory and research to support the claims that I make about reading educators like me and what we believe about how to teach reading in our schools.

Are Professors Like Me Ruining Our Schools?

Until early in 2014 I was a member of an on-line discussion group on Linked-In called "Literacy Leaders" which took up various questions related to literacy education like: "how to teach struggling readers"; "what are the best methods for teaching decoding?"; and, recently, "whether the 'reading wars' persist."

Until the discussion on the "reading wars" began in early 2014, I rarely took the time to read people's posts and I had never posted a comment of my own. But the "reading wars" topic interested me, so I read the initial posting which made some claims about reading educators whose perspective I shared – claims with which I disagreed. The author of the original post asserted, for instance, that literacy educators who took a more meaning-centered approach to reading instruction were "anti-phonics." The post also associated Ken Goodman, an eminent literacy scholar closely associated with meaning-centered approaches to reading instruction, with the so-called "whole word method" of reading instruction that emphasizes learning to read through the mastery of isolated sight words.

So I posted a comment to address what I saw as misunderstandings and mischaracterizations of "meaning-centered" approaches to teaching children to read. I wanted to make it clear that meaning-centered approaches to literacy education are not "anti-phonics." I wrote, for instance, that "no one reads with her eyes closed. Phonics is always part of the reading equation." I went on to say that:

> Advocates of meaning-centered approaches to reading instruction acknowledge a critical role for phonics but also hold that readers draw on other cues as they work to make sense of texts. Readers use their knowledge of sound-symbol relations in the process of reading but use this knowledge in concert with their knowledge of the regularities of language (syntax), and their knowledge of how the world works (semantics).

I also wrote that, contrary to the original posting on the reading wars, "Ken Goodman has never advocated teaching children to read through a whole-word method. Ken has written extensively that reading is a complex process in which readers draw on a range of cues in their effort to make sense of written texts. From Goodman's perspective, an over-reliance on word level instruction either through phonics or whole-word instruction corrupts the reading process." I'll say more about this shortly.

This rather innocuous posting – at least it seemed innocuous to me – provoked a furious reaction. People responded to my post by describing me as "the problem," and "the reason children in American schools are failing to keep up with their counterparts in high-achieving countries like Singapore and Finland." I read that I was representative of "whole language" professors who, some people argued, dominated reading education at American universities to the detriment of prospective teachers and, ultimately, the vast numbers of K-12 students who, it was claimed, are not able to read grade-level texts.

I chanced one more post. I wrote:

> I am not interested in polemics. I merely wanted to clarify the role of phonics in meaning-centered approaches to literacy education and Ken Goodman's relationship to whole-word

instruction. I want to make one more point. This will be my last post on this subject. The claim that "professors like me" are responsible for reading failures in this country presumes that meaning-centered approaches to reading education have been dominant in American schools. There is no empirical evidence to support this assertion. Nor is there any real evidence that "professors like me" dominate reading education in American universities. The claim that American school children are generally failing to learn to read also lacks any sort of research support. In fact, the evidence indicates that the vast majority of American children are learning to read quite well (for example, see Ravitch, 2013). The real issue is that children in poverty lag far behind their more affluent peers in learning to read. It also isn't clear that professors like me are the problem here since the evidence indicates that reading instruction in high-poverty schools emphasizes low-level (phonics) skills. In other words, meaning-centered approaches to reading may not be common in high-poverty schools.

This second post inspired another series of attacks on me and other "misguided" professors of reading education who are ruining America's schools. I don't really enjoy getting beaten up, so at this point I unsubscribed to this discussion group.

I was taken completely aback by the hostile, accusatory tone of these exchanges, but I guess I shouldn't have been. Lots of people, many with the power to affect educational policy, have concluded that the problem with reading education in this country is reading educators like me. One influential group that has been particularly harsh in its criticism of the way schools of education prepare teachers to teach reading is the National Council on Teacher Quality (NCTQ).

The National Council on Teacher Quality

The NCTQ was founded in 2000 and, according to its website, "advocates for reforms in a broad range of teacher policies at the federal, state and local levels in order to increase the number of effective teachers" (NCTQ, 2014). Educational historian and former Trustee of the conservative Fordham Foundation Diane Ravitch, offers a different perspective on the mission of NCTQ. According to Ravitch, NCTQ was founded by the Fordham Foundation "with the explicit purpose of harassing institutions of teacher education" (Ravitch, 2013). As I detail below, it seems that NCTQ has fulfilled this purpose quite well.

One of the NCTQ's earliest efforts to "harass" teacher education programs was a 2006 report on how reading is taught in university-based, teacher preparation programs (Walsh, Glaser, & Wilcox, 2006). The authors of the 2006 NCTQ report argued that they were motivated to look more closely at how reading is taught in schools of education by their suspicion that reading methods courses in teacher education programs were not attending to the call of the National Reading Panel (NRP) for "explicit, systematic teaching of phonemic awareness and phonics, guided oral reading to improve fluency, direct and indirect vocabulary building, and exposure to a variety of reading comprehension strategies" (Walsh, Glaser, & Wilcox, 2006, p. 3).

The NRP had been created by Congress to undertake a review of the available research on the teaching of reading (National Reading Panel, 1999). Although highly influential, there have been various interpretations of the NRP report, which has been criticized for its small sample sizes, its decision to exclude research studies that did not conform to the committee's narrow definition of "scientifically-based" research, and its general theoretical bias toward behaviorist models of reading that equate learning to read with the mastery of a finite scope and sequence of discrete skills (e.g., Garan, 2001).[2]

The authors of the 2006 NCTQ report began with the assumption that the findings of the NRP represented the final word on how reading should be taught, and then set out to determine the degree to which reading methods courses in schools of education embraced the "scientifically-based" principles of the NRP. To explore this question, the NCTQ undertook a "study" of reading courses at 72 American universities using course syllabi and required textbooks as indicators of course content. Based solely on an analysis of course syllabi and assigned texts in reading methods courses, NCTQ concluded that only 15% of the schools of education in their sample provided future teachers with even "minimal exposure" to the core components of the science of reading as determined by the 1999 NRP report (Walsh, Glaser, & Wilcox, 2006, p. 3).

Ultimately, the NCTQ report linked reading failures in the US to "faddish" reading instruction that, according to the authors of the NCTQ report, is unsupported by scientific research. The ultimate responsibility for reading failures among the nation's youth is laid at the feet of teacher educators like me who, the authors of the NCTQ report asserted, cling to "outmoded" theories and methods of reading instruction like independent silent reading and whole language that lack a (scientific) research base. Based on their findings, NCTQ then recommended that states implement a variety of policies and procedures to overcome resistance in schools of education to the "science of reading" (Walsh, Glaser, & Wilcox, 2006, p. 48). As the authors of the 2006 NCTQ report saw it, something needed to be done about teacher education faculty like me who were, in the minds of the authors of the NCTQ report, deliberately undermining the quality of reading education in this country.

I wouldn't claim that reading methods are taught effectively in all schools of education in the country. Nor would I argue that "teacher educators like me" can't improve the quality of their reading methods courses. I'm sure we can all do better. Still, I believe that the NCTQ's report on how reading methods are taught is too flawed to be taken seriously. For instance, making strong claims about the content of reading methods courses, particularly claims about the proportion of time devoted to particular topics, based on course syllabi is completely unjustified – and, ironically, completely unscientific.

The authors of the NCTQ report present no evidence that course syllabi are valid or reliable indicators of course content. My own syllabi give clear guidance on course assignments and topics I expect to cover in my courses, but my syllabi are poor indicators of the amount of time I will actually devote to various topics in my courses. Nor is there any reason to believe that course texts say much about what is and what isn't covered in particular reading methods courses since many instructors supplement assigned textbooks with other readings. I rarely even used a comprehensive textbook in my reading methods classes at Boston College. Instead, I had my students read numerous journal articles including articles summarizing empirical research studies – saving my students money in the process.

Oddly, the authors of the NCTQ report dismissed out of hand the possibility of contacting faculty or interviewing students on "methodological grounds," arguing that this kind of input would have undermined the objectivity of their study. Surely, it would have been useful to examine what actually occurs in reading methods courses in schools of education. But it seems that the authors of the NCTQ report weren't all that interested in what actually occurs in reading methods courses, since that would have interfered with their preconceived notions of how reading educators like me actually teach.

It's ironic that a report which valorizes scientifically-based reading research failed itself to meet the minimal criteria for quality research – especially the requirement that research measures what it claims to measure (i.e., validity). In addition to the shortcomings I have already discussed, the findings of the NCTQ study are not supported by any kind of third party (peer) review, a fundamental expectation for the publication of scientific research. Nor is there any reason to trust claims based on flawed data from 72 of the nearly 1200 university-based teacher preparation programs in the US. No wonder the Dean of the University of Iowa's College of Education concluded that the 2006 NCTQ report's "methodology [was] so flawed, none of us would accept it as a paper for a course" (Manzo, 2006, p. 12).

Yet, despite its fatal flaws, the NCTQ's claims about how reading is taught in American colleges of education was readily accepted by pundits and policy makers, no doubt because many already believed that there were serious problems with reading education in the US, and the principal reason was "liberal" professors of education like me.

NCTQ 2.0

In June 2013, NCTQ, in collaboration with *U.S. News & World Report*, produced another scathing report on the general state of teacher preparation in American universities concluding that schools of education "have become an industry of mediocrity, churning out first-year teachers with classroom management skills and content knowledge inadequate to thrive in classrooms with ever-increasing ethnic and socioeconomic student diversity" (NCTQ, 2013).

"Early Reading" is one of the five areas of focus of the NCTQ review. No one doubts the importance of preparing teachers who can teach reading well, so it must have been upsetting for teachers, parents, educational policy makers and the general public to read that, based on NCTQ's review of course syllabi and course textbooks, 71% of teacher preparation programs in the US are *not* preparing teacher candidates to engage in "effective, scientifically-based reading instruction" (NCTQ, 2013). This claim is, however, undermined by serious methodological problems with the NCTQ report.

To begin with, the *U.S. News/NCTQ's* findings on reading instruction in US teacher preparation programs include data on only slightly more than half of the teacher education programs in the country. This is a better sampling than the earlier NCTQ report on reading, but it is still uncertain if the schools sampled by NCTQ are representative of all schools of education. Certainly, many private universities, including my home institution of Boston College, suspicious of NCTQ's intentions and methodology, didn't comply with NCTQ's request for information.[3] Moreover, the report suffers from many of the same shortcomings as the earlier NCTQ report on reading, including the reliance on course syllabi and required textbooks as the indicators of course content and quality. The larger sample size did, however, permit NCTQ to produce state-by-state comparisons of how well, based solely on the judgments of NCTQ staff, US universities and colleges are preparing teachers to teach early reading.

Although NCTQ's conclusions are overwhelmingly negative, the authors of the NCTQ report did find considerable variation across states in how well teachers are being prepared to teach early reading. For instance, 64% of the teacher preparation programs in Louisiana and 60% of the programs in Mississippi were judged by NCTQ staff to be adequately preparing teacher candidates in effective, scientifically-based reading instruction. On the other hand, only 13% of teacher education programs in my home state of Massachusetts met NCTQ's standards for preparing students in early reading. Two other New England states, Maine and New Hampshire, had no institutions at all that met NCTQ's criteria for preparing teachers to teach reading.

As I read the NCTQ report, I couldn't help but notice that many of the states NCTQ ranked *high* in terms of the proportion of teacher education programs adequately preparing teacher candidates to teach early reading also ranked *low* on reading scores for 4th grade on the 2013 National Assessment of Educational Progress (NAEP, 2013). The NAEP bills itself as the "Nation's Report Card" on how well its schools are doing and, because NAEP assessments are administered uniformly using the same tests across the country, its results offer a useful metric for comparing students' performance over time and across states and districts. If the report of NCTQ is to be taken seriously as a valid assessment of how well teachers in any given state are prepared to teach reading, it seems reasonable to expect the NCTQ ratings to predict the performance of students on NAEP assessments. In other words, the quality of teacher education in a given state should have a predictable effect on student achievement.

In reality, there is a range of factors that affect reading achievement, including poverty, as I discuss later in this text. Teacher quality and, by implication, teacher preparation matter, but other factors matter, too. However, NCTQ's staff suggests that it is poor teacher preparation that is responsible for low reading achievement in the nation's schools. Given this position it is reasonable to expect a strong, positive relationship between NCTQ ratings in early reading and student reading achievement in given states. So it was somewhat surprising to see that my home state of Massachusetts, which ranks at the top on NAEP 4th grade reading scores for all 50 states, was rated so poorly by NCTQ in terms of how well its teachers are prepared to teach reading. Similarly, Maine and New Hampshire are among eight states that had no programs meeting NCTQ's criteria for early reading, but they also rank high on the NAEP 4th grade reading test. Conversely, Louisiana and Mississippi were ranked relatively high on NCTQ's early reading criteria, but are near the bottom of NAEP rankings for 4th grade reading scores.

This apparently inverse relationship between NCTQ's assessment of how well teacher preparation programs in various states are doing at preparing teachers to teach early reading, and the performance of students in those same states on the NAEP 4th grade reading test, led me and two of my Boston College colleagues, Marilyn Cochran-Smith and Larry Ludlow, to undertake a more systematic analysis of the relationship between the NCTQ rankings and the NAEP rankings. After all, the effectiveness of any teacher preparation program ought to be reflected in how well its graduates actually teach reading, which in turn should be reflected in students' performance on reading assessments like NAEP. But, again, the relationship between the effectiveness of teacher education programs and the success of students taught by graduates of particular teacher education programs is affected by a range of factors including poverty, the quality of curriculum and so on. I develop these points later.

Here's how we went about our analysis.[4] We first ranked all the states and the District of Columbia according to the proportion of programs in each jurisdiction that NCTQ concluded were effectively preparing teachers in "scientifically based reading instruction." We then created a rank ordering of the states and the District of Columbia according to the 2013 NAEP data for 4th grade reading (see data in the Appendix, Table 1). Utah, for example, sits at the top of the NCTQ rankings for programs meeting NCTQ's criteria for early reading, but ranks 30th for 4th grade reading on the NAEP.

Based on the NCTQ and NAEP's rankings we computed a correlation coefficient for the two distributions. This enabled us to determine the relationship between NCTQ's ratings for how well schools of education in individual states prepared future teachers to teach reading, and how well 4th grade students in that state actually performed on an objective measure of reading achievement. A positive correlation close to 1.0 would suggest a strong relationship between the NCTQ and NAEP rankings, validating the NCTQ findings as a good predictor of how effectively teachers actually teach reading in a given state. On the other hand, a correlation closer to zero would show the absence of a relationship between the NCTQ and NAEP rankings, indicating that the NCTQ evaluations are not a good predictor of teachers' effectiveness at teaching reading in particular states.

As it turned out, our calculations yielded a slight negative correlation of -.19 between the percentage of programs meeting NCTQ's criteria for early reading in each state and the District of Columbia and the NAEP rankings for those jurisdictions in 4th grade reading, as clearly shown in Figure 1.

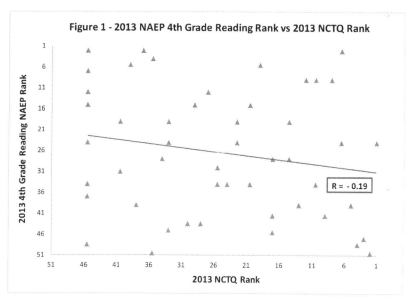

This simple analysis indicates no relationship between the proportion of teacher preparation programs meeting NCTQ's criteria for early reading in individual states and the reading performance of students in those same jurisdictions. In fact, there is a slight tendency for states ranked higher by NCTQ to have lower NAEP reading scores and states ranked low by NCTQ to produce higher reading scores among its 4th graders.

If NCTQ's evaluation criteria for early reading had any validity, we would expect at least a moderate relationship between the NCTQ ratings of how well teachers are prepared to teach reading in particular states and how well elementary students perform in reading in those same states. In other words, states like Massachusetts, Maine, and New Hampshire, whose teacher education programs were rated poorly by NCTQ, ought to perform relatively low on NAEP tests for 4th grade reading. And students in jurisdictions like Mississippi, Louisiana, and the District of Columbia, whose teacher education programs are favored by NCTQ, should to do well on NAEP reading. But, as it turns out, the opposite is true. In general, teachers in states whose teacher education programs are, by NCTQ's assessment, well prepared to teach early reading tend to get poor results compared to teacher preparation programs in states NCTQ concludes are not so well prepared. This is a bit of a conundrum for the folks at NCTQ. However, the meaning of this finding is clear to me. *Whatever the NCTQ is measuring, it seems to have little to do with how well teachers are actually prepared to teach reading.*

NCTQ asserts that its evaluation of teacher preparation programs provides useful information to parents of children looking to a career in teaching. According to NCTQ, parents and students should avoid wasting money on teacher preparation programs that do not meet NCTQ's criteria. The authors of the NCTQ report also argue that its findings should serve as a red flag to policy makers in states like Massachusetts whose colleges and universities failed to meet NCTQ's criteria for preparing teachers to teach early reading.

However, as it happens, the NCTQ ratings of programs in a given state predict the NAEP reading performance of students in that state no better than randomly pulling the NAEP scores out of a hat, and therefore have little use for parents, prospective students, or policy makers. The staff at NCTQ may be suspicious of university-based reading educators, but their data do not support their conclusions about professors like me and how effectively teacher educators in US universities and colleges are preparing the nation's teachers. Here's my recommendation for parents of high school students contemplating a career in teaching: save your money by not purchasing the issue of *US News & World Report* featuring NCTQ's evaluation of university-based teacher preparation programs. It won't help. To educational policy makers I offer the following advice. Yes, it is worth the time and effort to assess the effectiveness of teacher preparation programs. However, you will need to look elsewhere for guidance since NCTQ's assessments are without merit.

As I was writing this book NCTQ published its second annual *US News & World Report* evaluation of teacher preparation programs in US which I briefly examine in the following section.

NCTQ 3.0

The most recent 2014 NCTQ/*US News & World Report* mainly repeats the findings on early reading from the previous reviews. University-based teacher education programs are not adequately preparing future teachers to teach early reading, says NCTQ. Specifically, only 34% of university-based teacher preparation programs included in the NCTQ review either *meet* or *nearly meet* the NCTQ standard for early reading. Problems with the NCTQ procedures remain, however. NCTQ's evaluation of how well teacher preparation programs are teaching early reading is still based almost exclusively on reviews of course syllabi and course texts. And, once again, there is a negative relationship between NCTQ's evaluation of teacher education programs in individual states and student performance on the NAEP assessment of 4th grade reading (see data in the Appendix, Table 2).

For instance, NCTQ reported that 28% of the programs it reviewed in my home state of Massachusetts met or nearly met its early reading standard, but Massachusetts still ranks first overall on NAEP 4th grade reading scores among the states. NCTQ singles out Louisiana for having 100% of its teacher preparation programs meeting or nearly meeting NCTQ's standard for early reading, a result NCTQ credits to state policies to reform reading education in the state of Louisiana beginning in 2001. Yet, Louisiana's average NAEP score for 4th grade reading ranks 47th out of 51 jurisdictions (50 states and the District of Columbia). Additionally, only 23% of 4th graders in Louisiana met the NAEP reading standard for proficient or advanced compared to the highest ranked state, Massachusetts, where 48% of students met this standard. Similarly, NCTQ found that Connecticut, which ranks fourth overall in 4th grade reading on the NAEP, had only 11% of its programs that met NCTQ's criteria for early reading.

So once again I computed the correlation between these 2014 NCTQ ratings and the 2013 NAEP scores for individual states.

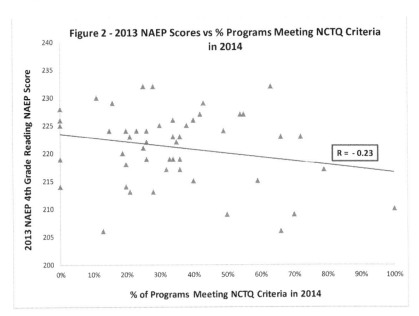

Because of how NCTQ reported its data I did the computation slightly differently this time, correlating the proportion of teacher preparation programs that met or nearly met NCTQ's early reading standard for each state with that state's NAEP 4th grade reading scores. As Figure 2 shows, this analysis yielded a slightly negative correlation of -.23, indicating no relationship between the NCTQ assessment of how well early reading is addressed in teacher preparation programs in individual states and how well students learn to read in that state.

There is one other issue with the most recent NCTQ report I wish to comment on. One complaint about the NCTQ evaluations has been the lack of transparency about the criteria NCTQ uses for evaluating teacher preparation programs. The most recent report is, however, somewhat clearer about the minimum requirements for meeting its early reading standard. Specifically, a course meets the NCTQ standard for early reading if it devotes at least two lectures to each of the five components of reading identified by the report of the 1999 NRP, and at least one assignment devoted to each component. This standard may be clearer but the criterion of two lectures plus one assignment for each component of reading is completely arbitrary. What of a course that requires extensive reading about phonics instruction but doesn't devote entire lectures to the topic? Why should it be necessary to discuss reading instruction in such a fragmented way, as opposed to discussing various components of reading together over the course of the semester? And why wouldn't an assignment (or test) that addresses multiple components of reading simultaneously be acceptable rather than assignments that address each component individually?

Of course, these questions speak to the limitations of NCTQ's use of course syllabi for program evaluation, including the assumption that different reading instructors use a common syllabus. Many (perhaps most) universities do not use common syllabi for their reading courses and it is completely unknown whether the syllabi evaluated by NCTQ are even representative of other syllabi at the same institution. I am fairly certain that the syllabus I used for the reading methods course I taught at Boston College would not meet (or even nearly meet) NCTQ's early reading standard, but the syllabi created by some of my colleagues teaching the same course at Boston College might.

The authors of the NCTQ report explicitly acknowledge *some* methodological problems with their review although they aren't specific about what they think those problems are. However, they argue that even with flawed methodology, the problems with university-based teacher preparation programs are obvious. I'm not convinced. For me, the absence of even a modest positive relationship between the NCTQ ratings of teacher preparation programs in individual states and reading performance of 4th grade students in those states destroys any claim of validity for NCTQ's evaluation of how well reading methods are taught in teacher preparation programs in the US. A flip of a coin would been an equally good predictor of how well graduates of teacher preparation programs in various states are actually teaching reading. In any case, the claim that the problems of teacher preparation programs were obvious to NCTQ even with flawed methodology makes it abundantly clear that NCTQ's conclusions fit neatly with their predetermined biases about teacher preparation in this country. To my eyes, NCTQ's evaluation of teacher preparation programs was largely an exercise in hand waving.

Why Reading Educators Like Me Resist NCTQ's Idea of "Scientifically Based Research"

A few years ago, my daughter Anne was looking for work and applied for a position with a national company that offers tutoring support for students in a range of school subjects including reading. As it happened, Anne was offered a job with this company in a phone interview that went something like this.

Company representative: Anne, tell us about your background and why you think you'd be a good fit for our company.

[Anne described herself and her background].

Company representative: Anne, we're impressed with your credentials and we'd like to offer you a job. But we know who your father is and we don't agree with his approach to teaching reading. If you're going to work for us you will have to teach reading our way, not his. If you can do it our way we'd like to have you work for us. Are you still interested?

Anne: You just insulted my father. I can't work for you.

[After a few pleasantries the conversation ended].

I was touched by Anne's loyalty but her phone conversation with the representative of the tutoring firm raised some questions for me.

What is it about the view of reading shared by professors like me that the tutoring company, like the authors of the NCTQ report and the folks who attacked me in the on-line discussion group, find so objectionable? Is the problem that professors like me are seen as "anti-phonics" and/or "anti-science" as the authors of the NCTQ report suggest? Are professors like me willfully ignoring the research evidence on the best practices for teaching reading? Is our willful ignorance really harming young children as the contributors to the Literacy Leaders discussion group suggested?

I believe that the fundamental beliefs about the reading process and the process of learning to read shared by meaning-centered reading educators like me have been misunderstood, mischaracterized, and misrepresented by our critics. No one is really "anti-phonics," for example. I also believe that the influence of reading educators like me on the way reading has been taught in our schools has been grossly exaggerated, as have the claims about the failures of the nation's schools to teach reading effectively.

In the next section I address the claim that reading educators like me are responsible for the supposed decline of reading proficiency in US schools. In the following Chapter 3 I explain what it is that reading educators like me actually believe about the reading process, and the research base for these claims. I also consider how NCTQ attempts to position university-based reading educators as illiterate consumers of reading research.

Finally, in Chapter 4 I contrast the goals of groups like NCTQ for reforming American education with the goals of reading educators like me.

Reading educators like me: "The reason children in American schools are failing to keep up …"

When someone posted on the "Literacy Leaders" listserv that reading educators like me were "the reason children in American schools are failing to keep up with their counterparts in high-achieving countries like Singapore and Finland" they were making two separate claims. First, US schools aren't adequately teaching children to read and, second, reading educators like me are responsible. This view is also implicit in the motivations and conclusions of NCTQ, as well as other critics of teacher education and US schooling more generally.

The evidence for the claim that US schools are failing to adequately teach reading is based largely on international comparisons and tests like NAEP that indicate that many children in the US fail to achieve above "basic" levels of competence in reading. Let me begin with NAEP scores.

The most recent NAEP (2013) results indicate that *only* 34% of fourth grade public school students tested were rated at or above "proficient reading." Critics have interpreted this to mean that barely a third of fourth graders in US schools can read at grade level (see Ravitch, 2013). Diane Ravitch, who served on the National Assessment Governing Board during the Clinton administration, points out, however, that it is a mistake to equate the NAEP category of "proficient" with acceptable grade level reading. Nor, according to Ravitch, is it appropriate to assume that "basic" means below grade level. Instead, Ravitch equates achieving a proficient level on the NAEP with an above average grade of B+, and achieving a basic level on the NAEP with a grade of B or C which, to me, sounds closer to average (or grade level). Additionally, the data also indicate that there has been a steady increase in 4th grade reading achievement since the NAEP was first administered in 1971 (National Center for Educational

Statistics, 2013). It would appear that, overall, US schools are doing a pretty good job teaching reading. But the key word here is "overall." A closer examination of NAEP scores does reveal a serious problem, however. Specifically, students living in poverty significantly underperform on the NAEP compared to more affluent students, and Black and Hispanic students do poorly relative to their White and Anglo peers (NAEP, 2013).

Critics of American teachers and the teacher educators who prepare them also point to international comparisons to support their claims that US schools are doing a poor job of teaching reading. Every three years since 2000, the Program for International Student Assessment (PISA) has measured the performance of 15-year-old students in various school subjects. In 2012 nineteen countries, including Poland and Estonia, had higher average scores in reading literacy than the United States and, overall, the average US score for reading literacy was no different from the average for the 34 countries that are members of the Organization for Economic Cooperation and Development (OECD) (National Center for Education Statistics, 2014).

It is easy to see how the overall performance of US schools in the PISA assessment of reading could be a cause for concern. However, David Berliner's (2013) analysis of data from international comparisons paints a much more complex picture. His analysis shows that US students attending schools with relatively low poverty rates do very well in international comparisons. He concludes that, "it is quite clear that America's public school students achieve at high levels when they attend schools that are middle- or upper-middle-class in composition" (p. 7). On the other hand, children and youth attending schools where more than 50% of the children live in poverty do not do nearly as well. Students attending schools where at least 75% of the student body is eligible for free and reduced price lunches do even worse. Berliner observes that in these schools "academic performance is not merely low: it is embarrassing" (p. 7). Nearly 20% of

American children attend these high-poverty schools. Berliner's analysis of international comparison reinforces the findings from the NAEP that children living in poverty, a disproportionate number of whom are Black and Hispanic[5], are not well served by American schools.

This is the real crisis in American education and, while I cannot claim to have an easy solution to this situation, I'm pretty sure that reading educators like me can't be blamed. To begin with, there is no evidence that the progressive (non-behaviorist) reading practices advocated by reading educators like me are common in high-poverty schools. There is, however, good reason to believe that the education of children in high-poverty schools, places overpopulated by Black and Hispanic students, is plagued by a "pedagogy of poverty" (Haberman, 1991) that focuses on low-level skills to the near exclusion of the engaging, high-level curriculum commonly found in higher academic tracks (e.g., Anyon, 1980; Oakes, 2005). In reading instruction this typically takes the form of curriculum focused on "basic" reading skills (e.g., phonics, phonemic awareness) (Allington, 2000; Finn, 2009). For instance, the demand that *Reading First* schools[6] rely on "scientifically-based" reading instruction was routinely translated into a focus on low-level, basic skills (Gamse, Tepper-Jacob, Horst, Boulay & Unlu, 2008).

The rationale for emphasizing low-level skills in high-poverty schools is that these children need to master the basics if they're going to be effective readers. But students learn what they are taught and, conversely, students do not learn what they are not taught (Allington, 1983); therefore, students in schools and classrooms emphasizing basic, low-level reading skills are taught – and learn – very different academic content. These students learn the skills of reading but are routinely denied opportunities to engage in challenging, higher-level reading practices (Finn, 2009). So it's not surprising that children who are subjected to a nearly exclusive emphasis on low-level reading skills in the early grades tend to experience a decline in reading performance around 4th grade (the 4th grade reading slump) when there is a greater emphasis on reading comprehension (Chall & Jacobs, 2003). This likely accounts for the finding that, "children living in high-poverty areas tend to fall further behind [in reading], regardless of their initial ... skill level" (Snow, Burns & Griffin, 1998, p. 98), a finding that led James Gee (2004) to ask:

> What is it about school that manages to transform children who are good at learning ... regardless of their economic and cultural differences, into children who are not good at learning, if they are poor or members of certain minority groups? (p. 10)

Curriculum matters, and I believe that children in poverty – and struggling learners more generally – are best served when they are provided with the rich, challenging curricula common in affluent, high-achieving schools and classrooms.[7] Research on de-tracked schools demonstrates how well low-achieving students respond to challenging curricula (e.g., Oakes, 2005; Watanabe, 2008). Still, more challenging curriculum, while necessary, will be insufficient to overcome out-of-school factors that limit the educational opportunities of students living in poverty. Research on student achievement shows that teachers – and by implication, teacher educators – are not the most important influences on student achievement. In fact, most research indicates that less than 30% of a student's academic success is attributable to schools, and teachers are only part of the overall school effect, perhaps not even the most important part (Berliner & Glass, 2014, Location 1258)

On the other hand, Berliner noted that:

> Out-of-school variables account for about 60% of the variance that can be accounted for in student achievement. In aggregate, such factors as family income; the neighborhood's sense of col-

lective efficacy, violence rate, and average income; medical and dental care available and used; level of food insecurity; number of moves a family makes over the course of a child's school years; whether one parent or two parents are raising the child; provision of high-quality early education in the neighborhood; language spoken at home; and so forth, all substantially affect school achievement. (Berliner, 2013, p. 5)

To further test the relationship between poverty and reading achievement, I computed the correlation between the percentages of children living in poverty in each state (as reported by the National Center for Children in Poverty, 2014) with 4th grade reading scores by state on the 2013 NAEP (see data in the Appendix, Table 3). As Figure 3 clearly shows, this analysis yields a correlation coefficient of -0.67 (NAEP scores decrease as poverty level increases), a remarkably high correlation given the range of factors that can affect academic achievement.

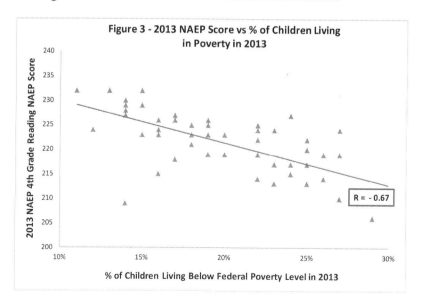

Louisiana, which NCTQ singled out in its 2014 report for having 100% of its teacher preparation programs as meeting or nearly meeting its standard for early reading and, as I noted above, was near the bottom for 4th grade reading scores on the NAEP, is tied with New Mexico for the second highest proportion of children living in poverty among all states. While I am critical of NCTQ's evaluation of teacher education programs I have no doubts about how hard Louisiana teachers and teacher educators are working to overcome the debilitating effects of childhood poverty in that state.

I believe that the evidence supports reading educators like me, who reject reading instruction overly focused on low-level skills like phonics and phonemic awareness in favor of more challenging, meaning-based reading instruction. This raises the question: what do reading educators like me believe about the teaching of reading? I tackle this question next in Chapter 3.

What Reading Educators Like Me Believe and Do Not Believe About Reading – And Why

Let me be clear from the outset. Reading educators like me – that is, reading educators who work from a meaning-centered perspective – DO NOT reject the "science of reading" as has been claimed by NCTQ and others. However, we do reject the model of reading implicit in the NCTQ report, as well as reading research that builds on this same model of reading. Let me begin by sharing my perspective on the model of reading that informs NCTQ and most other critics of meaning-based reading instruction.

The view of the reading process and how children learn to read that underpins the NCTQ report as well as the report of the NRP (1999) is based on a discredited (behavioral) model of human learning (see, for example, Chomsky, 1959). The fundamental assumption of this model of reading and reading instruction is that written language is based on an alphabetic code.

It works like this. Writers encode their message using the conventions of English orthography in which particular combinations of marks on the page (or screen) represent letters that, in turn, represent sounds that are joined into words. Readers then draw on their knowledge of letters and letter-sound relationships to "break the code" as a means of recognizing words quickly and accurately thereby translating written language into oral language as a means of decoding the author's meaning. Essentially, this model of reading equates learning to read with the mastery of a finite scope and sequence of skills (letter recognition, sound blending, etc.). From this perspective, instruction focuses on teaching students to:

- Recognize letters
- Learn that letters are associated with particular sounds
- Learn that words can be broken into component sounds or phonemes
- Rapidly and accurately blend sounds into words (i.e., fluency)

The basic assumption here is that once young readers have achieved an optimal level of fluency, reading comprehension, the ultimate goal of reading, happens more or less automatically as readers translate the marks on the page to oral language. The critical role of fluency in this model can be seen in the widespread use of fluency measures in reading assessments in US classrooms. The Dynamic Indicators of Basic Early Literacy Skills (DIBELS) measure of oral reading fluency (total number of words read accurately in one minute), for example, is among the most widely used measure of early reading in our schools. There is some sense to this given the primacy given to fluency in behavioral models of reading. Fluency is conceived of differently in other models of reading, however.

When students don't learn to read as quickly or as efficiently as expected, the assumption of those working from a behavioral perspective is that students are *deficient* in the underlying skills assumed to be associated with competent reading. Remediation, when deemed to be necessary, focuses on systematically (re)teaching these skills, often through a form of behaviorally-oriented, direct instruction.

There are, to be fair, different versions of this behavioral/developmental model of reading, some much more complex than what I've described here. More complex behavioral models highlight, for example, various cognitive, metacognitive, and dispositional traits and abilities that are presumed to be involved in the reading process such as attention, perception, memory, phonological processing, motivation, and so on. What these models have in common with the simple behavioral model of reading I described above is the linking of the reading process and learning to read with *underlying* skills and abilities. Behavioral models of reading also share a heavy, sometimes exclusive, emphasis on word level skills in beginning reading instruction.

The appeal of behavioral models of reading and learning to read lies, I imagine, in their relative simplicity, familiarity and association with the notion of "scientifically-based" research embedded in the reports of the NRP and the NCTQ. Reading as a process of decoding is easy to understand and, since most people's school experience included a heavy emphasis on phonics, it's likely that policy makers, politicians, teachers, parents, and members of the general public believe that they learned to read *because* of phonics instruction.

There is, however, an uneven relationship between what teachers do and what students learn. Teachers may teach phonics and students may learn to read but that does not mean that students learned to read *because* teachers emphasized phonics. That correlation does not imply causation is a basic axiom of educational research. Behavioral models of reading, because of the emphasis on discrete, measurable skills, also fit well with popular understandings of scientifically-based educational research that focus on measurable human behaviors. From a behavioral perspective, human behaviors, even complex behaviors like reading, can always be broken down into component (measurable) parts. Reading research has tended to focus on measuring these *parts* to measure the efficacy of various interventions; however, in doing so, researchers necessarily situate their research in a behaviorist model of reading.

Despite their simplicity – maybe *because of* their simplicity – I don't find behaviorist models of reading convincing. Nor am I persuaded by reading research based on flawed behaviorist models of reading. It is not, however, just a matter of being opposed to phonics, explicit instruction, or even "scientifically-based" research. It's that I just don't believe behaviorist models of reading capture the incredible complexity of the reading process. This is my problem with behaviorist theories of human learning in general. Human learning is much too complex to be accounted for by simplistic behaviorist theories.

Rejecting behaviorist models of reading does not mean that professors like me are opposed to phonics, explicit instruction in various aspects of the reading process, or "scientifically-based" research (an oddly redundant phrase). Caricatures of reading educators like me as anti-phonics, anti-explicit instruction, and anti-science are unfair and untrue. I know of no reading educators, including the most zealous whole language advocates, who do not acknowledge a crucial role for phonics in reading and learning to read. The print is always part of the process. How could it not be? The issue isn't *whether* to teach phonics or not, but *how*, *when* and *why* we should teach phonics. I'll say more about this later.

Reading educators like me also take for granted that *all* students require some measure of explicit support and direction as they learn to read and write. Laissez faire teaching, expecting students to learn to read simply by reading without explicit support from their teachers, is, quite simply, bad teaching. When I teach or write about reading methods for teachers I always emphasize that young readers require varying degrees of "intensive, explicit, and individualized support and direction" from their teachers (Dudley-Marling & Paugh, 2004, p. x). The notion that there are reading educators who believe that teaching reading is just about putting out the books and letting kids learn to read *naturally*, as some critics suggest, is patently absurd.

Finally, reading educators like me do not reject "scientifically-based" research. We do, however, dismiss reading research built on a discredited behaviorist theory of learning that fails utterly to account for the complexity of human behavior. Good research isn't just about sound methodology, it must also be based on good theory. It is, therefore, reasonable to reject a body of research if it built on flawed theory. Let me expand on this point.

All research – whether in psychology, biology, physics or reading methods –is undertaken from some (theoretical) point of view. In the case of reading research, all methodological decisions made by researchers, including the measures chosen to determine the effectiveness of various interventions and the interpretation of results, are influenced by researchers' predetermined beliefs about reading and the nature of the reading process. For example, a substantial body of research on reading focuses on measures of word-level skills (e.g., phonemic awareness, sound blending, fluency) to test the effectiveness of different approaches to reading instruction. Reading researchers working from this perspective are, however, rarely explicit about the theory of reading that informs their research. But, again, all research is undertaken from some point of view.

A colleague tells the story that he once heard a leading reading policy expert claim that he had "no theoretical perspective." The claim that reading research can be undertaken from no particular perspective is nonsensical. This is not to claim that researchers are unreasonably biased, but only that they are human, and we humans always apprehend reality from some perspective. Without some shared (cultural) perspective nothing would make sense. Even the hard sciences are undertaken from a theoretical perspective, a theory of how the universe operates (see, for example, Kuhn, 1962). For instance, the instruments aboard Mars rovers that are designed to search for evidence of life are based on some theory of what extraterrestrial life forms might look like. Should life exist that falls outside of astrobiologists' conceptions of life, it will be invisible to the rovers' instruments. The design of the rovers' instruments is saturated with theory and so is the design, execution, analysis and interpretation of reading research. It cannot be otherwise.

Implicit in the focus on word-level skills as measures of *reading* is a behaviorist model of reading that equates the mastery of skills and sub-skills with learning to read. Those of us who reject this research paradigm are not hostile to scientific research. We just don't accept the simplistic behaviorist model of reading that animates much reading research, including the reading research privileged by the NRP[8] and valorized by the NCTQ. Instead, we favor approaches to reading research that capture the infinite complexity of the reading process. Put simply, I reject behaviorist models of reading and reading research based on these models because I find more complex, sociocultural perspectives on what it means to read and how children learn to read more persuasive. I share this view with many other (perhaps even most) university-based reading educators.

In the following section I discuss sociocultural models of reading and reading instruction.

A Sociocultural Theory of Reading

One of the hallmarks of sociocultural models of reading – and learning more generally – is that these theories draw on a wide range of theoretical influences. To illustrate some of the influences of sociocultural models of reading, I'll try to describe the various influences that have shaped my own (sociocultural) view of reading.

My first exposure to reading methods was when I entered a one-year, special education teacher preparation program at the University of Cincinnati in 1970. I remember making a "phonics wheel" for one of my courses that students could use to make different words (f-at, c-at, etc.) by turning the wheel which exposed different consonants (onsets) on the outside of the wheel that combined with syllables (rimes) (e.g., "at," "ar," "it" and so on) written on the inside of the wheel. This activity fairly well characterizes the nature of reading methods in my program at UC. I was taught that teaching reading was a matter of selecting from a menu of activities for teaching prerequisite skills and subskills presumed to be fundamental to learning to read.

This was a quintessentially behaviorist approach to teaching reading, underpinned by the assumption that all learning can be broken down into sets of skills and sub-skills. As it turned out, my first teaching position was in a school for children with intellectual disabilities (IQs under 50), where it was taken for granted that students lacked the cognitive capacity for learning to read. Still, in my fifth year of teaching, spurred by a teaching aide who had been trained as an elementary teacher, we began teaching reading to many of our students with some success. Research over the past 20 years has proven how completely wrong we were in initially assuming that our students could not learn to read (Buckley, 2012). They can – and did thanks to my enlightened aide – although children with intellectual disabilities may well have difficulty learning the meaningless, low-level skills we (wrongly) assumed were fundamental to learning to read (Kliewer, 2008).

Although I wasn't thinking much about reading pedagogy early in my teaching career, I did give a lot of thought to learning, which inspired me to read lots of books by and about Piaget. Piaget's theories of learning provided a sharp contrast to the behaviorist perspectives that dominated both my special education training and my undergraduate work in psychology at the University of Cincinnati. Piagetian inspired research demonstrates that human learning cannot be reduced to sets of atomized skills and, most importantly, Piagetian research shows that what children learn is a function of what they already know.[9]

For example, at a particular point of my daughter's development her concept for "dog" included all four-legged animals and, for a time, all she learned about four-legged animals was *assimilated* into her schema (roughly, a Piaget notion for concept) for "dog." Over time, she created new schemas for different four-legged animals as a means of *accommodating* her concepts to her experiences. In this formulation, learning is a reciprocal process in which learners take in (assimilate) new information that is understood in terms of current schema while simultaneously transforming existing schemas in order to accommodate new experiences (data). The constructivist principle that people learn through the lens of their experiences remains fundamental to my understanding of human learning and the processes of reading and learning to read.

Around the same time, I took a series of courses on language acquisition from Professor Richard Kretschmer, a brilliant teacher at the University of Cincinnati. What I learned about theories of language and language acquisition in this course became foundational to my thinking about oral and written language. This is where I first learned, for example, what amazing language learners all children are. Typically, children become functionally adult speakers by age four when they are immersed in rich language learning environments that include caretakers who both model language *and* respond to children's language use in ways that ensure that it works – that is, children learn the language they need to in order to function in their social and cultural contexts.

In Richard's course I also learned about the complex theories of language acquisition developed by Noam Chomsky and others to account for children's extraordinary linguistic accomplishments. I particularly recall reading Chomsky's (1959) seminal essay, "A review of B.F. Skinner's Verbal Behavior," which thoroughly dismantled behaviorist theories of language acquisition (and, arguably, behaviorism more generally). Chomsky observed, for example, that children produce new and novel utterances that they've never heard before based on their own tacit theories of language (e.g., "I runned to car.").

My doctoral work in sociolinguistics at the University of Wisconsin beginning in 1978 reinforced this sense of language as a system far too complex for behaviorist theories to account for. For example, from a sociolinguistic perspective, children don't just learn about words and word ordering rules. They learn a mind bogglingly complex set of rules for varying both what they say and how they say it, according to whom they are addressing, in what social and cultural context, and for what purpose.

More recent sociolinguistic research also illustrates the complex ways people make different linguistic choices to position themselves and others (Gee, 2012; Fairclough, 1989). One of the primary uses of language, for instance, is to claim membership in various social and cultural groups. I make very different choices, for instance, when I assume the role of professor than I do when taking on the identity of sports fan, bicyclist, father, or even husband (see Gee, 2012). Language is also used to reinforce power and privilege, as in the case of sexist language that seeks to position women as powerless relative to men. Even the language choices of very young children tend to reinforce the relative status of language users based on age (and, all too often, gender). Again, it is difficult to see how a behaviorist theory of language, which necessarily conceives of learning in terms of discrete skills and abilities, can account for the richness and complexity of language in real world use.

My introduction to meaning-centered theories of reading also came courtesy of Richard Kretschmer. Anticipating my interest in reading instruction, Richard suggested to me several books by progressive reading educator and theorist Frank Smith. In Smith's view, children are meaning makers extraordinaire for whom making sense is fundamental to their motivation to learn, including learning to read (Smith, 1973, 1988/2006).

Smith argues that breaking down learning to read into meaningless bits and pieces actually makes learning to read much more difficult, because it deprives children of their natural sense-making abilities (1979/2011). Children can and do learn the "skills" of reading, Frank Smith says, but in contexts where these skills are part of the process of making sense of texts.

It was also about this time that I attended a lecture by Carolyn Burke, a widely respected professor of reading education at Indiana University. Carolyn explained reading miscue analysis to her audience by sharing illustrative examples of students' reading miscues. Children's reading errors – or miscues – offer insight into how readers approach the reading process, specifically the different sorts of information (or cues) they use to make sense of texts in the process of reading (Goodman, 1973), and the degree to which they are guided by the desire to *make sense*. Miscue research shows, for example, that efficient readers don't just sound out words but use their knowledge of the sound system of language (graphophonics) in concert with their knowledge of the structural regularities of language (syntax) and their knowledge of how the world works (semantics) as they work to make sense of what they're reading.[10]

Miscue research demonstrates that reading is not a linear process of decoding letters and words, as readers often scan the text looking for syntactic and semantic cues – and sometime non-textual cues like pictures or other images – to help them make sense of texts, a finding confirmed by eye-movement research (Paulson & Freeman, 2003). If good readers produce miscues that don't make sense – that is, are syntactically or semantically inappropriate – they tend to correct them, confirming that effective readers are, above all else, motivated to make sense. From this perspective, reading problems are defined as an overreliance on one cueing system, often to the exclusion of sense making. For instance, readers who focus their attention mainly on graphophonic (sound-symbol) cues to the exclusion of syntactic or semantic cues will tend to have difficulty making sense, because meaning always goes beyond letters, sounds, and words.

Consider the example (adapted from Carolyn's Burke's talk) of a boy who began reading *The Three Little Pigs* "The first little big made a horse out of string." What do we make of the three miscues, *big*, *horse* and *string*? Some might take the "b" for "p" substitution as evidence of a perceptual problem associated with dyslexia. And "horse" for "house" and "string" for "straw" might be seen by some as evidence of a young reader who got the first sounds of each word correct but then just guessed the rest, suggesting the need for more intensive phonics instruction.

However, someone working from a meaning-based perspective (like Carolyn Burke) would point out that the reader in the above example produced a text that first, made no sense, and second, ignored the reader's own experience in the real world. It would appear that the reader was motivated more by a desire to get the words right than actually making sense of what he was reading. Specifically, the sentence the reader produced is ungrammatical (the "first little big" what?) and nonsensical despite the near certainty that the story of the three little pigs was familiar to him.

Good readers produce miscues all the time, but they tend to correct them when they don't make sense. And good readers always draw on their background knowledge as they construct meaning from texts. In other words, good readers are focused on making sense of text using a wide range of cues while poor readers tend to be focused on sounding out words without any particular regard for sense-making. To be sure, there are poor readers who give insufficient attention to sound-symbol relationships, but this is less common in my experience. But, again, I want to be absolutely clear that this is not an "anti-phonics" position. Phonics matters. Readers cannot ignore the words on the page. The problem is an overreliance on phonics in the process of reading connected text.

Reading educators who work from a sociocultural perspective are persuaded by overwhelming evidence that reading is a process of making sense in which readers draw on all available cues as they construct meaning from texts. But we do not believe that the evidence supports the claim that there is a single, unitary process for making sense of texts. It follows logically that equating reading with the mastery of an autonomous set of reading "skills" will always be insufficient to understanding the reading process (Street, 1995). The readers' purpose and background knowledge, the social and cultural setting, the nature of the text, and so on all affect how readers interact with texts.

As linguist James Gee (1990) puts it, readers don't learn to read "once and for all" as much as they learn to read particular texts (e.g., religious texts, novels, operating instructions, webpages), for particular purposes (e.g., participation in religious rituals, gathering information, to be entertained, studying for tests), in particular settings (e.g., church, school, coffee house, basement workshop, virtual space). Participation in a religious ritual, for instance, often involves reading from a text, but "reading" is more than simply getting the words right. For the religious practice to achieve its meaning requires the right people (priest, minister, Imam, rabbi, congregants) interacting with the right text (e.g., prayer book) in just the right way (standing, kneeling, heads bowed, prostrate) in the right time and place (a church, not a tavern). "Reading" the text in any other way will fail to achieve its significance (meaning).

Similarly, the meaning of reading in the context of a book club or a shared reading of the newspaper at the kitchen table depend on following entirely different sets of conventions, which vary according to the social and cultural context. Even solitary reading loses its significance if undertaken at the wrong time or place. In many families solitary reading is a highly valued practice associated with individual success, but is generally discouraged at places like the dinner table or at certain times in school. And some sorts of solitary reading are more highly valued than others. Parents and teachers are more likely to value classic fiction and non-fiction texts over comics or graphic novels, for example. And in certain cultural settings solitary, independent reading may not be valued at all, as some families may view reading alone as a rejection of social obligations to family members.

Reading practices associated with "doing school" (e.g., round robin reading, phonics worksheets, getting the main idea and so on) must also be performed in just the right way to *count* as reading. The familiar practice of round robin reading (small reading groups in which students take turns reading from a common text with teachers giving support as students read), for example, is more than getting the words right. Successfully doing round robin reading requires that students follow along while other students are reading so they'll know where to begin reading when it's their turn (or at least giving the impression of paying attention), not interrupting other students, following the teacher's lead and so on. Research by Ray McDermott (1976) illustrates how failure to perform any of the actions associated with round robin reading is sufficient to get labeled a poor reader. When I worked as a learning disabilities teacher in Green Bay, Wisconsin I sometimes worked with students who read fluently but had difficulty completing phonics worksheets. So I helped them learn the reading practice of completing worksheets.

There are a couple of important points I'm trying to make here. First, there is much more to effective reading than getting the words right. Reading is about participating in complex cultural practices and learning to read is as much – and perhaps more – about learning to participate in these practices as getting the words right. But – and this is the crucial point – the only way to learn how to *read* for a range of purposes, settings, and intended audiences (that is, participate in a range of reading practices) is by being immersed in these various practices. No child learns to read "once and for all" because there is no unitary set of skills that works in all contexts. The reading practices students learn in school, for example, work best in school settings, but will not automatically transfer to other sorts of literacy. This is a particular problem in high-poverty schools and special education classrooms where there is a nearly exclusive focus on word-level skills that have little currency beyond the walls of schooling. And even within the walls of schools, an over emphasis on word-level skills (learning to read) will not prepare students for the demands of content area reading (reading to learn) (Chall & Jacobs, 2003).

The second point I'm trying to make is about where the *meaning* of texts resides, which has clear implications for how we teach reading. The common sense view, informed by most people's experience in schools and behaviorist models of reading, is that meaning is encoded *in* the text waiting to be decoded by the reader. The very word *decode* implies that the goal of reading is to decipher some underlying meaning in the text that has been *encoded* by an author. But, from the sociocultural perspective that informs the work of reading educators like me, the meaning of texts is in the social practice as a whole and, in any case, texts themselves never have unambiguous meanings. Even the meaning of something as seemingly straightforward as a stop sign is relative to its placement (we're likely to ignore a stop sign in the middle of a block as misplaced), who is driving and for what purposes (emergency vehicles always aren't expected to observe stop signs), and what they're driving (bicycles don't always observe stop signs even if they should), and so on.

Viewing reading as a set of social practices dramatically affects how we think about the meaning of texts in another way. Texts are always interpreted within a cultural frame of reference based on shared meanings by members of cultural groups. Language is, arguably, the primary means by which we interpret texts, but this isn't an individual act of meaning making. We share the meanings of words with other members of our cultural group, and without a shared cultural reference point there is no meaning – unless you believe that readers can make sense of texts from no point of view at all. That, to me, makes absolutely no sense. Readers also make sense of texts through the lens of their experiences. When I read any text I do so from the perspective of a privileged, white, aging male, former academic, and a person with a particular set of experiences, values and beliefs.

This brings me back to the constructivist theories of Piaget whose research convincingly demonstrates that new learning is necessarily a function of what individuals already know. Similarly, no two readers can ever get precisely the same meaning from any text, since no two readers have identical sets of experiences. This does not mean, however, that anything goes in the interpretation of texts. Readers are expected to produce "responsible readings" (Rosenblatt, 1994) that don't do violence to writers' intentions, yet always draw on the reader's background knowledge and experience as part of the process of meaning construction. It wouldn't be acceptable for a reader to see the pigs in the *Three Little Pigs* as the aggressors, for example, but we would expect individual readers to assign different understandings to what it means for the pigs to lose their homes.

As Rosenblatt (1994) describes it, reading is a complex interaction – she calls it a "transaction" – between writers who draw on various print-based resources to fulfill some intention with an imagined audience, and readers who draw on their own linguistic resources, experiences, and intentions to bring meaning to a writer's text. A successful "transaction" satisfies the intentions of both writers and readers, but rarely results in the transfer of unambiguous meanings. From a sociocultural perspective, writing and reading are both active, meaning-making processes that go well beyond encoding and decoding texts.

A Meaning-based Perspective on the Teaching of Reading

In the preceding section I tried to explain briefly the theories of learning and theory of reading that inform how I taught reading methods to my students at Boston College, and how I taught reading during my eight year career as a classroom teacher. Many, perhaps most, university-based reading educators share these theoretical perspectives, including reading educators associated with the unfairly maligned "whole language" movement. In general, reading educators like me assume that meaning, not decoding, is the key to reading and learning to read. Again, this doesn't mean that we are anti-phonics as the members of the Literacy Leaders listserv charged.

Some readers might be thinking that reading theory doesn't really matter and it was unnecessary to explain the theoretical perspective that informs my work with students. What matters, they might say, is effectively teaching children to read regardless of theory. I agree – sort of. Ultimately, all reading educators want to prepare teachers who are thoroughly grounded in the best practices for teaching reading. And we certainly want best practices to be informed by rigorous research. But determining what counts as a "best practice" is a function of both good research *and* sound theory. Educators should never be convinced by shoddy research, nor should they be persuaded by research – no matter how well executed – that is based on faulty theory.

I am persuaded that the research base for behaviorist based reading instruction in this country, the same research base that informed the NRP and the reports from the NCTQ, is seriously flawed simply because the behaviorist theory of reading that underpins this research is so flawed. Behaviorist theories do not – and cannot – explain the incredible complexity of ordinary human behavior, including learning to read.

Sociocultural theories of reading, on the other hand, do account for the complexities of (socio)culturally-situated human behavior, including learning to read and write. I am also persuaded that there is a solid (and growing) research base for this perspective.[11]

Much of this research was ignored, however, by the NRP which accepted only experimental and quasi-experimental studies that favor the measurement of the low-level, discrete skills that characterize behaviorist models of reading. Such measures are, however, ill-suited to complex, sociocultural theories of reading. How, for example, would you measure the degree to which readers use the range of available cues for constructing meaning from texts or how they use non-linguistic information for making meaning? This knowledge *can* be assessed, but not through narrow approaches to research that focus on "countable" behaviors.

This all begs the question: what does a sociocultural theory of reading look like in practice? In what follows, I'll try to give an idea of what best practices look like from a sociocultural perspective by outlining what I take to be some basic principles for teaching reading. Sociocultural theories of learning lack the "measure and test" simplicity of behaviorism, but I'll do my best to describe what a sociocultural approach to reading instruction looks like, through the lens of a set of principles that underpinned how I taught reading myself as an elementary teacher, and how I taught future teachers about reading instruction.

1.   The Ultimate Goal of Reading Is Making Sense

As I learned from Frank Smith (1973) over 40 years ago, making sense of texts is fundamental to reading instruction from the beginning. Children don't learn to read (i.e., decode) and then learn to make sense. Young readers learn to use visual information, among other cues, as part of the sense-making process. From an instructional perspective, this means young children reading – and being read – "authentic" texts that were written to be read, as opposed to contrived texts that were written to teach narrowly focused decoding skills (think: "The big frog sat on the log") and, therefore, make little sense.

Certainly it is useful for students to learn about the regularities of English spellings, in this case onsets and rimes or "word families" (e.g., fat, bat, cat, sat, etc.). However, an overemphasis on meaningless bits of print removed from the context of reading whole texts only makes learning to read more difficult by depriving learners of their natural sense-making abilities (Smith, 2006). It also misrepresents what readers actually do in the process of reading connected texts. Keeping written language meaningful by focusing on "whole" (uncorrupted) texts is the real meaning of whole language. Stripping away the meaning from early reading instruction also risks future problems by persuading some children that the point of reading is merely getting the words right, not making sense. As a classroom teacher I worked with lots of struggling readers whose primary problem was that they read letter-by-letter, word-by-word without any attention to context or meaning and, as a result, produced readings that were nonsensical. This brings me to the next principle.

2. Readers Make Sense of Texts by Drawing on A Range of Linguistic and Visual Cues

Effective readers draw on their knowledge of language, their knowledge of the world, *and* their knowledge of sound-symbol relationships in the process of reading. It is insufficient to merely sound out words without attention to meaning, but it also won't do for readers to rely too heavily on other cueing systems. Readers can't, for instance, just make up stories based on pictures or other cues without reference to the words on the page. Therefore, reading educators like me share with prospective teachers a range of strategies to get young readers to simultaneously use the full range of cueing systems to make sense of texts *including the use of phonetic cues.*

3.   Phonics Matters

I've already addressed this point in the previous principle but I want to be clear here since reading educators like me are frequently accused of being anti-phonics. To be absolutely clear, <u>no one reads with their eyes closed</u>. Effective readers MUST (and do) make use of the (visual) marks on the page to make sense of any text. How much they rely on phonics depends on a number of factors including text difficulty, the reader's background knowledge, purpose, and so on. The issue isn't phonics per se, but the degree of emphasis readers place on phonetic cues.

For example, teachers working from a behaviorist perspective may feel justified focusing exclusively on getting the words right as a prerequisite to fluent reading (and, presumably, meaning making). In contrast, reading educators working from a sociocultural perspective teach students to use phonetic cues in the presence of other cueing systems. In other words, learning to read isn't about learning to use phonics in isolation, but learning to use phonetic cues in concert with syntactic and semantic cues in particular social and cultural contexts. The evidence indicates that effective readers use as much visual (phonetic) information as they need to make sense of texts. For example, in the sentence, "The boy hit the ball with the bat" readers need minimal visual information to figure out "bat" (or even "ball") given the presence of linguistic and contextual cues. Again, how much visual information to focus on will depend on the context of reading. But, to be crystal clear, no reading educator believes that phonics isn't part of the reading equation.

4.   A Different Take on Fluency

From a behaviorist point of view, fluent reading is a matter of reading rapidly and accurately, evidence of efficient sound blending required for accurate comprehension. Reading educators working from a sociocultural perspective also value fluent reading, in part because dysfluent reading (choppy, hesitant reading) forces readers to over-rely on letter-sound information to the exclusion of syntactic and semantic cues, and also because fluent, expressive reading is evidence of reading comprehension. Strategies like repeated reading (repeatedly reading the same text), assisted reading (reading along with young readers), and sustained silent reading are powerful tools for developing reading fluency in beginning readers.[12]

5.   Students Must Be Immersed in Print

Effective reading teachers immerse their students in literacy. They create classrooms brimming with all sorts of reading (and writing) materials including books of all kinds, fiction, non-fiction, poetry, folk and fairy tales, memoirs, graphic novels and so on. A literacy rich classroom also includes magazines, comic books, joke books, and student-written work. Students may also have access to a range of digital texts (webpages, news sites, etc.). And there is lots of environmental print (e.g., signs, directions, schedules, lunch menus, various lists, comics, etc.). Classrooms rich in reading materials invite students to engage in extended reading, while at the same time they demonstrate to students the purposes of reading (Smith, 1981). Of course, a rich literacy learning environment is only effective if students have regular, extended opportunities to read independently (and be read to by their teachers). Regrettably, there is evidence that many students may have few extended opportunities to engage in independent reading in school (Gallagher, 2009).

6. **Students Must Have Regular Opportunities to Read Independently**

Put differently, reading is fundamental to reading development. This should seem pretty obvious but for many children, particularly those who are deemed to be "at risk" for school failure, there is often a hyper focus on low-level skills that leaves little time for students to actually read real texts. In some cases, young learners are kept away from books until they have fully developed their reading skills (e.g., phonics, phonemic awareness) on the assumption that actual texts (which include words that do not follow simple phonics rules) will confuse them. More often there just isn't time provided for children to read authentic texts in school. Many schools have ceased providing time for independent reading, citing the report of the NRP which indicates that there is insufficient experimental evidence to draw any firm conclusions about the efficacy of independent reading.

There is, however, an impressive body of correlational research (oddly, the NRP dismissed correlational research) which indicates a very strong relationship between the amount of reading children do in and out of school and their development as readers (Allington, 2011; Krashen, 2013). Allington (2011) puts it very simply: the more words students read the better they will develop as readers. When I was a third-grade teacher I provided my students with 45-50 minutes of independent reading time every day. While my students were reading independently I worked with children individually and in small groups to provide targeted reading instruction based on my ongoing assessment of their reading development.

7. Students Need to Read a Range of Text Types

This relates to the previous principle and builds on an earlier claim that children don't learn to read "once and for all" but, instead, learn to read particular texts in particular ways for various purposes (Gee, 1990). The point here is that learning to read one genre – fiction, for example – is insufficient preparation for reading other genres (non-fiction, poetry, memoir, etc.).

Students need regular opportunities to read various text types that place different demands on readers – for example, reading a non-fiction text to prepare for a test is quite different from reading poetry for personal pleasure. Increasingly this includes digital texts like web pages that follow a very different logic from traditional text types. None of this is meant to suggest, however, that reading educators like me believe that students will learn to read without the explicit support of their teachers – which brings us to the next principle.

8. All Readers Need Some Measure of Explicit, Intensive, and Individualized Support and Direction

This principle may surprise some readers. Reading educators like me have often been pilloried for our presumed belief that learning to read, like learning to talk, is "natural" and, therefore, there is no need for explicit instruction (see, for example, Groff, 1996; Mock & Kauffman, 2004). Just put out the books and children will learn to read. It is true that I, like many other reading educators who privilege meaning making over low-level skills, believe that learning to read and write are similar in many ways to learning to talk. We believe, for example, that learning to read (or talk) requires immersion in meaningful, purposeful (reading) behaviors supported by adults who model skilled language use and provide appropriate feedback. But this falls well short of claiming that learning to read is a "natural" process or asserting that learning to read and learning to talk require the same sort of support from adults. More to the point, I know of no reading educator who claims that teachers should refrain from providing explicit instruction to beginning readers. Not one.

My own work with teachers, including books and articles I've written for teacher audiences (e.g., Rhodes & Dudley-Marling, 1996; Dudley-Marling & Paugh, 2004), has always been clear about the need for explicit and individualized instruction. All readers require some measure of explicit instruction targeted to their individual needs, and some readers require more frequent and intensive explicit instruction than others. I'd go even further and argue that laissez-faire teaching – the failure to provide explicit instruction when needed – is evidence of incompetence. The issue isn't whether explicit instruction is necessary. It is. The issue for reading educators like me is our objection to reading instruction focused nearly exclusively on the explicit teaching of low-level skills removed from meaningful engagement with authentic texts.

As a 3rd grade teacher[13] I routinely provided my students with explicit instruction in reading strategies and skills in the context of brief whole class, small group, and individualized mini-lessons, based on my routine assessment of students' needs.[14] For instance, I conducted daily, whole-class spelling mini-lessons in which we playfully examined regularities of English orthography (e.g., the silent *e* in in words like "same" typically marks the vowel as long, double consonants in words like "batting" generally mark the vowel as short and so on).[15]

Similarly, as my students read aloud individually for me during our independent reading time, I sometimes asked them to sound out words by breaking the words down into syllables, perhaps covering parts of the word with my thumb as they sounded out each syllable. I frequently used these opportunities to talk about some of the general rules that govern English orthography. Sometimes I did brief cloze (fill in the blank) exercises e.g., "The man hit the ball with a _____", to encourage students to use context cues as they read. We also talked about whether the texts they produced in the process of reading made sense or not.[16]

These are just a few examples of the explicit instruction that was routine in my 3rd grade classroom. But I always tried to keep the focus on meaning making in the context of reading authentic texts (books, magazines, etc.). Importantly, I provided explicit instruction informed by my assessment of my students' individual needs, not instruction based on some general, one-size-fits-all curriculum targeted to an imagined "average" student. Teachers shouldn't waste time teaching students things they already know or aren't ready to learn, something I see quite frequently when I visit schools.

9.   Making Sense Does Not Mean Getting THE Meaning

The fundamental goal of reading instruction is to make sense by fulfilling the intentions of readers and writers. This is *not* the same, however, as the rapid and accurate reading of individual words, which proponents of behaviorist models of reading equate with "proficient" reading. In most contexts, reading miscues (e.g., omissions, substitutions) that don't substantially affect meaning don't matter (e.g., reading "home" for "house").

Proficient readers make many miscues, and there is no need to correct students' miscues if they don't do violence to the meaning. If miscues do significantly affect the meaning, skilled readers – unlike weaker readers – revisit their miscues and correct them. So, if readers produce miscues that don't make sense, reading educators like me don't correct them, but instead draw students' attention to the need to read "sensibly."

10. **All Children Can Learn to Read.**

All but the most seriously disabled children can learn to read, although not all children will achieve the same level of reading success. As I discussed earlier, evidence over the last 30 years makes it clear that that even children with moderate intellectual disabilities can and do learn to read (Buckley, 2012; Kliewer, 2007). Some children will, however, require more frequent, intensive, explicit and individualized support and direction from their teachers as they learn to read. This is certainly the case for students with intellectual disabilities. Interestingly, as I noted earlier, there is evidence that, while children with intellectual disabilities can learn to read actual texts, they may have difficulty learning isolated skills like phonemic awareness (Kliewer, 2008). This is only a problem if you presume that low-level reading skills are prerequisites for developing higher level reading practices – a position that reading educators like me explicitly reject.

11. **The Above Principles Don't Change Because a Child Has Acquired a Label**

Many children with disabilities, children whose first language is not English, and children who come to school with less experience with books than their peers, will all likely require more frequent, intensive, explicit and individualized support and direction than their peers. But they do not require unique instruction. There are no special reading methods for individual children because of some educational classification such as Learning Disabled (LD), autistic, or English Language Learner (ELL). At least there shouldn't be. Reading educators like me believe that the emphasis on low-level reading skills typical in schools and classrooms where children are presumed to be "different" is a primary reason poor readers fall further and further behind as they pass through the grades regardless of their level of reading when they enter school (Snow, Burns & Griffin, 1998).

For many children the material effects of poverty are an even more obvious cause of school failure. Children in high-poverty schools and special education classrooms are seriously disadvantaged by behaviorist approaches to reading instruction that emphasize low-level skills to the near exclusion of opportunities to engage with books, the most important element in any successful reading program. This does not mean that I expect all children will achieve the same level of success in reading. Some children will take longer to learn to read, and not all children will achieve the same level of reading skill.

One problem with the Common Core State Standards (CCSS) is the assumption that *all* children should be able to read at the highest levels. For instance, one of the CCCS English Language Arts standards for elementary grades indicates that "by the end of the year" children in third grade will independently read text at "the high end of the grades 2-3 text complexity band" (National Governors Association Center for Best Practices, Council of Chief State School Officers, 2010). It is utterly absurd to suggest that *all* children can learn to read above grade level, i.e., at the high end of the grades 2-3 "complexity band". Worse, this expectation ensures that many children – and consequently their teachers – will be considered failures. Educators like me favor high expectations in the form of opportunities for all students to engage thoughtfully with challenging texts, but not the expectation that all students can achieve at "above average" levels of achievement, which is a statistical impossibility.

12. Effective Teachers of Reading Draw on Their Professional Knowledge and Experience to Teach Reading

Teaching is a complex activity that cannot be reduced to scripted lessons, standardized curricular materials, or one-size-fits-all programs (Allington, Johnston, & Day, 2002). So-called "proven" programs only work in the hands of expert teachers who either modify them significantly or abandon them altogether, based on careful, ongoing assessment of the needs of individual learners (Allington, 2002). In this context, critical factors in the teaching-learning equation are teachers' professional discretion, informed by their content and pedagogical knowledge (including knowledge of theory and research), their teaching experience (including their experience with the individual children in their classrooms), and systematic inquiry into their own practices (see Cochran-Smith & Lytle, 2009).

So what teacher educators like me aim for is to graduate prospective teachers who are knowledgeable about reading theory and research, and who are ready to begin teaching. We do not expect that our graduates are fully formed teachers of reading, because experience and professional development really matter. To paraphrase eminent reading educator Yetta Goodman, a reading teacher isn't something one becomes as much as something one is always in the process of becoming. This is supported by research indicating that teachers are most effective after several years of classroom teaching experience (National Commission on Teaching and America's Future, 2010; Rice, 2003). This point is evident to anyone who has been a teacher, but is not so obvious to so-called educational reformers who typically have little or no classroom teaching experience.

13. Teachers Should Be Held Accountable for Student Learning but Not Test Scores

Corporate educational reformers emphasize teacher accountability as a key to improving student achievement. Reading educators like me also believe that teachers should be held accountable for their teaching. The question isn't *whether* teachers should be held accountable but *how*. Many so-called reformers want teachers to be accountable for students' scores on standardized tests, but this method of accountability is highly problematic since, as I noted earlier, other factors critically affect student scores on these tests. Teachers cannot single handedly overcome the effects of poverty, chronically underfunded schools, or ineffective, prescriptive curricula focused on low-level skills.

But if teachers cannot be held accountable for student test scores what should they be accountable for? Here's my take on teacher accountability: I believe that teachers should be able to show parents and administrators what their students have learned, and that they have done all they can to push every student in their classroom as far they can go as readers. And, if students struggle learning to read, teachers should be able to show what they did differently – e.g., modify and/or intensify reading instruction – to tailor instruction to their assessments of students' learning needs. I suspect most parents would prefer this sort of accountability instead of simple scores on standardized tests that provide little to no information about their children's learning potential.

14. Teacher Educators Should Be Accountable for What Their Students Learn, Too.

Reading educators like me welcome accountability for preparing teachers who are knowledgeable about reading theory and practice. We want our students to be prepared to be effective teachers of reading, but we also expect our students to continue to grow as teachers through routine reflection on their practice and professional development. We want our graduates to be able to talk about student learning and how they provide instruction appropriate to students' assessed needs. However, we reject efforts to link student test scores to the universities their teachers graduated from as a means of assessing the effectiveness of individual teacher education programs, as NCTQ does, for instance.

First of all, as I noted earlier, teachers are *not* the most significant factor in student learning, nor are teacher preparation programs necessarily the most important factor in teacher effectiveness. The influence of teacher preparation programs is diminished, for example, when teachers work in under-resourced, high-poverty schools plagued by prescriptive curricula that provide little room for teachers' to exercise professional discretion that research has shown to be crucial to teacher effectiveness (Allington, Johnston &

Day, 2002).

If graduates of the teacher education program I worked in at Boston College end up working in schools that employ heavily scripted approaches to reading instruction, it's difficult to see how their course work in reading could make much of a difference in their teaching. Nor can the most effective teacher education programs prepare teachers to single-handedly overcome the material effects of poverty. This point raises an even bigger worry about linking student achievement to teacher preparation programs.

As a group, students in high-poverty schools score poorly on standardized tests, and they typically demonstrate less annual growth on tests than students attending more affluent schools (Berliner & Glass, 2014). Therefore, teacher preparation programs whose graduates tend to work in districts serving low-income students will be at a significant disadvantage compared to teacher education programs whose graduates work mainly in more affluent school districts. A system that evaluates teacher preparation programs based on students' test scores in the schools in which these graduates teach will have the effect of punishing schools of education that encourage their graduates to teach in the neediest schools.

This sort of system will almost certainly encourage many teacher educators to push their graduates away from low-achieving, high-poverty schools where they are most needed. The appeal of a value-added system for assessing teacher preparation programs lies in its apparent simplicity. But simple systems for evaluating the incredibly complex

relationship between an individual student's reading ability and teacher preparation programs, teachers, school
funding, curriculum, students' background and so on will
certainly fail.

The fourteen principles I've outlined above are fundamental to how
I taught future teachers during my 33 years as a teacher educator, and to
how I taught children when I worked as a classroom teacher. I believe
that most university-based reading educators share these views. As a
group, we do not ignore reading research, as the folks at NCTQ claim.
What we reject is reading research and instruction based on flawed
behaviorist models of learning, particularly learning to read. We have a
different view of reading and reading instruction from that of the authors
of the various NCTQ reports and other so-called educational reformers,
including the people on that polemic Literacy Leaders listserv. And, as
I've tried to show above, our views on reading and reading instruction
are supported by both theory and research reinforced by our experience
as classrooms teachers.

Reading Educators as Producers of Knowledge

The basic conclusion of the authors of the various NCTQ reports, the
members of the Literacy Leaders listserv, and other critics of university-
based teacher education is that the nation's teachers are failing to teach
reading effectively and that the problem is reading educators like me
who, it is claimed, willfully ignore the scientifically-based research on the
teaching of reading as summarized by groups like the NRP. I attempted
to debunk these claims in previous chapters and sections arguing that,
on balance, US teachers do a good job of teaching reading. The issue is
that students attending high-poverty schools fail to reach expected levels
of reading achievement compared to students in more affluent settings.
But the difficulties of teaching students in high-poverty schools go well

beyond the adequacy of teacher preparation programs. Like all teacher educators, I want the very best teachers implementing rich, engaging curriculum for all students attending high-poverty schools; however, this will never be sufficient to overcome the myriad of problems that plague high-poverty schools, including the material effects of poverty, chronic underfunding, pedagogy focused on low-level skills, and so on.

Critics of university-based reading educators are right about one thing though. Many reading educators who work from a sociocultural perspective do reject the "science of reading" embodied in the report of the NRP because, as I argued earlier, it is based largely on a discredited (behaviorist) model of reading and how children learn to read. The NRP report is further undermined by a host of conceptual and methodological problems (e.g., Garan, 2001; Krashen, 2001). To many critics of university-based teacher education this must seem like incredible hubris. Who are we to challenge the scientific authority of the NRP report, for example? Or even the work of the NCTQ?

The authors of the NCTQ reports attempt to position teacher educators as "consumers" of reading research whose job it is to faithfully pass on to prospective teachers the collective wisdom of the "scientists" who produce reading research. From their perspective, ignoring the science of reading is an act of ignorance that perpetuates fads like whole language that critics argue "lack a research base" – meaning that they aren't endorsed by the NRP.

The reality is that university-based reading educators are not *mere* consumers of research. Overwhelmingly, the reading research that is presented at academic conferences and published in the most prestigious journals, including the behaviorist-oriented research that underpins the report of the NRP, is produced by faculty in the schools of education at our nation's universities. Similarly, the critical theoretical work on what it means to "read" and the processes of learning to read has mainly been produced by scholars in university schools of education. To be sure, not all teacher education faculty are expected to do research, but even then, most teacher education faculty have earned doctoral degrees, and therefore possess the training and skills necessary to conduct and evaluate research.

Teacher educators possess an additional qualification that helps them in both conducting and interpreting reading research. With rare exceptions, teacher educators are experienced classroom teachers, and in most cases, continue to work in schools in support of teachers and students. Therefore, teacher educators understand the complex practice of teaching in the tangled spaces of actual schools and classrooms, and they are well positioned to undertake and interpret reading research. They also recognize that reading research conducted in isolated or controlled settings outside the messy realities of schools and classrooms has little relevance for classroom teachers. Overall, the work of teacher educators like me, which lies at the intersection of theory and practice, qualifies us well to evaluate reading research.

What NCTQ and Other Reform Groups Want/What Reading Educators Like Me Want

So far, my defense of reading educators has focused on pedagogical issues, that is, what reading educators like me believe about the teaching of reading, and the theoretical and research support for those beliefs. I've also tried to rebut claims by NCTQ and other critics about, first, the supposed "failures" of US schools, and second, that teacher educators are responsible for many children not learning to read as well as we would like them to.

But, at its heart, this is much more than a simple pedagogical debate. Yes, for some people this is an honest difference of opinion about the most effective methods for teaching reading. However, in general, the underlying disputes about the effectiveness of teachers and the teacher educators who prepare them represent ideological divisions about the meaning and purposes of schooling in a participatory democracy, including the purposes for teaching reading. Patrick Shannon, the eminent reading educator and critical theorist at Penn State University, has long argued that, ultimately, attacks on schools and teachers are part of a larger political struggle over the purposes of schooling in a modern democracy. So it's important to consider the political implications of debates over the teaching of reading in American schools.

In the following section I briefly explore the ideological stance that

I believe animates high profile critics of American schooling. I then discuss my own ideological commitments which I believe I share with other reading educators working from a sociocultural perspective.

What Reformers Want

The NCTQ website notes that the organization was founded "to provide an alternative national voice to existing teacher organizations and to build the case for a comprehensive reform agenda that would challenge the current structure and regulation of the profession." Toward this end, NCTQ says that it "advocates for reforms in a broad range of teacher policies at the federal, state and local levels in order to increase the number of effective teachers."

This is what they say but, consistent with Diane Ravitch's observation that NCTQ was founded by the conservative Fordham Institute "to harass teacher preparation programs," the work of NCTQ and its staff has functioned mainly to antagonize and discredit teachers and the teacher education programs that prepare them. If NCTQ was primarily motivated to help improve the quality of teacher education, they could have sought partnerships with accreditation agencies or groups like the American Association of Colleges of Teacher Education (AACTE), a national alliance of teacher preparation programs. They haven't.

If NCTQ was truly interested in enhancing the quality of individual teacher preparation programs they could easily have sought some form of cooperation with schools of education. They most certainly have not. Similarly, if NCTQ was really interested in improving the quality of teacher preparation in US colleges and universities, they would have adopted a transparent system for evaluating teacher preparation programs that at least had some validity. As I believe I demonstrated above, the use of course syllabi and assigned textbooks to evaluate the quality of reading methods courses in teacher education programs has no relationship to how well teachers actually teach reading or how well they are prepared to teach reading.

Further evidence of NCTQ's position on teacher education is the makeup of its Advisory Board which, as Marilyn Cochran-Smith notes in her foreword to this text, is a veritable who's who of people known for their antagonism toward traditional public schools and university-based teacher education in particular (e.g., Frederick Hess, Wendy Kopp, E.D. Hirsh, Joel Klein). NCTQ's donors also include many groups and organizations that have been less than supportive of traditional, university-based teacher preparation programs, including the Bill and Melinda Gates Foundation that donated nearly $11 million to NCTQ between 2009-2013 (Hassard, 2013; Bill & Melinda Gates Foundation, 2015). But NCTQ's efforts to reform teacher education is just one part of a larger political project that aims to discredit public services, including K-12 schools and public college and universities, as a first step in "reforming" (or "*de*forming" as Marilyn Cochran-Smith put it in her foreword to this text) schools and other public institutions (Babones, 2015).

Educational reformers' antipathy toward publically funded and operated schools – what some critics pejoratively label "government schools" – can be traced to a free market (also called neoliberal) theory of political economy which holds that the well-being of individuals can best be advanced "by liberating individual entrepreneurial freedoms and skills within an institutional framework characterized by strong private property rights, free markets, and free trade" (Harvey, 2005, p. 2).

From this point of view, the role of government is limited to providing safety and security to its citizens, while avoiding any regulation that interferes with the efficient operation of markets. Moreover, governments are expected to leave to the markets the provision of services, including utilities, transportation, and education, that, it is argued, could be more efficiently – and profitably – delivered by the private sector (Harvey, 2005).

Economist Milton Friedman (1955), one of the most influential advocates of privatizing government services, argued that the most effective means for reforming American education would be to expose schools to the competitive forces of the free market. To accomplish this goal, Friedman proposed that vouchers be made available to all parents who could use their vouchers to send their children to any school of their choice. Free market advocates like Friedman begin with the assumption that competition provides a powerful incentive for schools to be efficient and effective, in contrast to traditional public schools that, as monopolies, have no such incentive. The presumption is that in a competitive environment, the best schools will thrive and ineffective schools will literally go out of business. Friedman also believed that the profit motive would lead to the emergence of a variety of schools to meet parents' demand for quality education. In such a system the state's role would be limited to ensuring that schools meet minimum standards, but otherwise allowing the invisible hand of the free market work its magic without the interference of government.

For a variety of reasons, the idea of reforming schools through the use of vouchers never gained much traction in the United States. However, the fundamental idea behind Friedman's voucher proposal, that giving parents *choice* would subject schools to the competitive forces of the free markets, thereby leading to better and more effective schools, has become the dominant theme in educational reform. The claims of economists such as Chubb and Moe (1990) that opening up educational markets to competition is a necessary *and* sufficient condition for reforming American schools reflects the view of many contemporary educational reformers. Here's how Chubb and Moe put it:

We think reformers would do well to entertain the notion that choice *is* a panacea.... It has the capacity all by itself to bring about the kind of transformation that, for years, reformers have been seeking to engineer in myriad other ways. (p. 217)

It is this thinking that underpins the rapid proliferation of charter schools in the United States[17], a trend that enjoys the support of both Republicans and Democrats, including senior education officials in the Obama administration (Ravitch, 2010).

Many critics of traditional models of public schooling seem to believe that opening up schools and other public services to the competitive forces of the free market will provide the magic bullet that will solve intractable problems like the persistent underachievement of students in high-poverty schools. There is a quasi-religious belief in the power of markets to make everything right. But not all of those advocating for market solutions to educational problems are motivated by ideology. Many see US public education budgets "as pots of gold to be mined for private gain" (Babones, 2015). In a Reuters article from 2012 Stephanie Simon observed that:

> The K-12 market is tantalizingly huge: The U.S. spends more than $500 billion a year to educate kids from ages five through 18. The entire education sector, including college and mid-career training, represents nearly 9 percent of U.S. gross domestic product, more than the energy or technology sectors.

For-profit charter schools, cyber schools, and voucher programs are already generating enormous profits, without much accountability or even evidence of effectiveness (Berliner & Glass; Molnar, 2015; Ravitch, 2013). For instance, the last several years has seen the rapid expansion of highly profitable, online cyber schools, many operated by private educational management organizations. Indeed, the cyber schooling industry is projected to have revenues approaching $25 billion by 2015 (Berliner & Glass, 2014). Currently, thirty-seven percent of cyber schools were operated by a single for-profit entity, K12 Inc. (Molnar, 2015). Yet, compared to traditional brick-and-mortar schools, virtual schools serve relatively few poor students, Black and Hispanic students, or students with disabilities. Significantly, cyber schools also lag far behind traditional public schools on adequate yearly progress (AYP), state rankings and graduation rates (Molnar, 2015).

The potential for profit also explains investors' interest in charter schools, an investment sector that is estimated to grow at a rate of 12 to 14 percent a year (Jackson, 2015). The growth of charter networks around the US offer new revenue streams for investing as well as significant tax breaks for those who invest in charter schools in underserved areas (Singer, 2014). Additionally, the real estate industry "also stands to benefit by promoting charter schools and helping them buy up property, or rent, in inner city communities" (Singer, 2014). Even charter schools operated by non-profit boards "are essentially pass-through front operations for profit-making companies" (Babones, 2015).

Similar trends are apparent in teacher education. For instance, online teacher education may be the fastest-growing sector of teacher preparation, and is a market dominated by for-profit groups (Sawchuk, 2013). Even within traditional teacher education programs, the evaluation of student teachers is being outsourced to publishing giant Pearson Education, a company that generated profits in excess of $1.5 billion in 2011 (Singer, 2012). Currently, there are 616 teacher preparation programs in 35 states and the District of Columbia participating in Pearson's Teacher Performance Assessment (edTPA) (American Association of Colleges for Teacher Education, 2015).

It is no wonder Sirota (2013) concludes that "the most significant lesson from the ongoing debate about American education has little to do with schools and everything to do with money." For many so-called reformers, profit is the prime motivation.

Still, the public and policy makers need to be persuaded to abandon traditional public schools, and convincing American to embrace market-based alternatives to traditional public schools is being accomplished mainly through a relentless attack on public schools, teachers, and teacher educators. Perhaps the opening salvo in the campaign to discredit public education in the US was the publication of *A Nation at Risk*, commissioned by Ronald Reagan, a strong supporter of school vouchers. The authors of *A Nation at Risk* argued that the general mediocrity of American schools was threatening the national security of the United States by undermining the competitive position of the US in the global economy (National Committee on Excellence in Education, 1983). Since then there's been a steady barrage of damning critiques of schools and teachers aimed at undermining support for traditional public schooling. As Rupert Murdoch (2011) put it in a commentary published in *The Wall Street Journal*, "we must approach education the way Steve Jobs approached every industry he touched. To be willing to blow up what doesn't work or gets in the way."

NCTQ's negative reports on the state of teacher education are just another piece of a "manufactured crisis" (Berliner & Biddle, 1995) that has provided fertile ground for initiatives like *No Child Left Behind* (NCLB), that dictate a range of market-inspired reforms. These include "accountability, high-stakes testing, data-driven decision making, choice, charter schools, privatization, deregulation, merit pay, and competition among schools" (Ravitch, 2010, p. 21). The current trend toward standardization, homogenization and frequent assessment provides the data consumers need to make informed choices regarding their children's schooling. Ultimately, the current crop of school reformers seeks to remake public schools in the image of the free market, while "open[ing] up public education to a massive transfer of public funds to corporations" (Lipman, 2007, p. 51).

The all-out assault on public institutions is worrisome enough, but neoliberal, free market ideology extends beyond business principles and profit motives to encompass all forms of human interactions, even the meaning of democracy. Here's how Lipman (2007) puts it:

> Neoliberalism reframes all social relations, all forms of knowledge and culture in the terms of the market. All services established for the common good are potential targets of investment and profit-making. In the discourse of neoliberalism, the society becomes synonymous with the market, democracy is equated with consumer choice, and the common good is replaced by individual advantage. (p. 51)

Free market ideology eliminates the concept of the common good and community and replaces them with the ethic of individual responsibility (Martinez & Garcia, 2000). This philosophical position animates attacks on labor unions, anti-poverty programs, and health care mandates, for example, since individuals are conceived as autonomous actors who do best when they take care of their own needs (Hursh, 2007) without the intervention of government.

> While personal and individual freedom in the marketplace is guaranteed, each individual is held responsible and accountable for his or her own actions and well-being.... Individual success or failure are interpreted in terms of entrepreneurial virtues or personal failings (such as not investing significantly enough in one's own human capital through education). (Harvey, 2005, pp. 65)

In this context, school failure is reduced to a lack of individual ability and effort and, in a market free of government interference – i.e., forcing children to attend public schools – making poor choices among available options for schooling. This last point deserves an additional comment. In the context of free-market schooling, if parents choose to send their children to schools that ultimately turn out to be ineffective – as many charters have (Ravitch, 2010) – well, that's their fault for making poor choices. This logic undercuts critics of free-market schooling, who argue that the poor performance of many charter and voucher schools demonstrates the need for increased government regulation of these schools. In the logic of neoliberalism, if the free market fails to produce the desired results – in this case, create more effective schools – it is the fault of consumers for not making good choices.

Fundamental to free market beliefs is the assumption that the individual is an "autonomous entrepreneur responsible for his or her own self, progress, and position" (Hursh, 2008, p. 65). Concepts like community and common good are anathema to free market ideology because, in theory, they restrict the individual's freedom to make informed choices on their own behalf. It is in this context that libertarian politicians assert that government mandated health care, food assistance programs, welfare, and even social security are threats to individual freedom. In this formulation, social justice merely requires that individuals be given access to markets and, if they fail to achieve educational and economic success, they only have themselves to blame (Hursh, 2007).

Ultimately, neoliberalism frames individuals as mere cogs in larger economic structures. In this marketized version of civil society "consumer rights increasingly come to prevail over citizen rights" (Whitty, Power, & Halpin, 1998, p. 46). The role of schools is to prepare students for the workplace, and this is best accomplished when schools are freed from the burdens of government regulations that, it is claimed, limit individual choice. The value of the individual lies in her or his potential contributions to the economy, and reading and other school related subjects are merely commodities, skills to be exchanged in the marketplace. President George W. Bush was widely mocked for saying that, "You teach a child to read, and he or her will be able to pass a literacy test" (Bushism, n.d.). But in the logic of the marketplace this makes perfect sense since the literacy test certifies students as "workplace ready".

Ultimately, happiness, satisfaction, fulfillment and the common good have little currency in a free market formulation of society, beyond the base assumption that equates human fulfillment with economic success. This dystopian, every-person-for-themselves vision of American society is an anathema to reading educators like me, who are all committed to the notion of a common good that supersedes the selfish interests of the individual. I explore this position in the following section.

What Progressive Reading Educators Want

Statistically, the United States is a remarkably diverse country popu-lated by people from a myriad of cultures, religions and races, speaking literally hundreds of different languages. The evidence also indicates that the US is becoming even more diverse with time. According to the US Census Bureau (2015), by around 2020 more than half the nation's children are expected to be part of a "minority" race or ethnic group, and by 2060 only 36% of all Americans under 18 years of age will be "single-race non-Hispanic white." Yet, despite our nation's increasing diversity, there is reason to worry that many Americans may actually have fewer opportunities to interact with people different from themselves.

For example, after decades of racial integration in our schools, more recent patterns indicate a troubling re-segregation of American schools, particularly high-poverty, urban schools (Kozol, 2006). To drive this point home, as I'm writing this paragraph I'm sitting in the teachers' lounge of a Dorchester elementary school in Boston where nearly all the faces are black or brown. Other urban schools I visit in places like Boston and New York look much like this. Of course, this reflects housing patterns and disproportionately high levels of poverty in Black and Hispanic communities, a serious problem in its own right.

Further, there is a trend for Americans to choose to live in communities of like-minded people (Bishop, 2009), a pattern reflected in the wildly different views on various social issues in different regions of the country, and even in cities within states and neighborhoods with cities. Americans seem to be sorting themselves into enclaves of people who think and look like themselves. This trend, should it continue, threatens a core principle of a participatory democracy, one that ensures the rights of all citizens, even those in the minority. How do we respect the rights and beliefs of our fellow citizens if we are isolated from one another? Certainly it is easier to fall prey to pernicious stereotypes of the poor, the rich, Muslims, Evangelical Christians, and gays and lesbians, for instance, if we have no contact with members of these groups.

Arguably, one of the most important functions of public schooling is to give each of us opportunities to meet each other, and to develop mutual respect and understanding across cultural, ethnic, religious and socioeconomic groups. Americans like to believe that underneath our differences we share our American-ness, marked by a particular vision of democratic life. But with relatively few opportunities for meaningful interactions with people different from ourselves, the political culture in the US is increasingly plagued by a self-absorbed tribalism devoid of empathy for the lived experience of our fellow citizens.

For example, it is easy to believe that the lives of poor children are deficient in the cognitive, linguistic, emotional, and spiritual resources needed to escape poverty (Payne, 2005) if we have no meaningful interactions with people living in poverty. It is no wonder that deficit thinking – focused on what's wrong with children and families living in poverty – is the dominant lens for viewing children who struggle in school. Assuming that there is something wrong with poor children, children whose first language isn't English, Black and Hispanic children, and children with disabilities, without respect for their language, culture and experiences, we then proceed to try and "fix" them, a fundamentally disrespectful act.

I used to ask my Boston College students which of them actually knew someone who was poor and typically no hands would go up. These were future teachers who we expect to respect the backgrounds and experience of all their students. But how do they respect the experiences of children whose lives are mostly foreign to them? It's not impossible, of course, and I'd like to believe that, overwhelmingly, the prospective teachers I worked with at BC are good and caring people. But I fear it will be difficult for them to create respectful, caring, inclusive classrooms if they have little understanding of the lives their students live outside of school.

This is about more than pedagogy, however. Undermining the institution of school as a public good further erodes any sense of collective identity or responsibility for people different from ourselves. Worse, the competitive individualism at the heart of market-based schooling offers no motivation for caring about the lives of our fellow citizens, beyond outperforming them. For some neoliberals, the free market is not just a way of organizing our schools, but a way of organizing our society. In this formulation consumerism replaces citizenship as the fundamental democratic value. Poverty is not our problem. People just need to work harder. Racism, sexism, homophobia. The markets will take care of it. Selfishness is good for the markets, and dispositions like empathy are for losers.

Teacher educators like me firmly reject this dystopian, everyone-in-it-for-themselves vision of schooling and society. A society organized by the free market is a lonely, hateful place that is an anathema to caring teachers eager to create respectful, inclusive classrooms.

In the end, those who seek to discredit traditional public schools, teachers, and teacher education programs to pave the way for market-based reforms have a thoroughly different vision of the purposes of schooling – and the purpose of teaching students to read – than teacher educators like me. Unlike advocates of market-based schooling, teacher educators like me believe that the purpose of schooling is to prepare thoughtful, interesting, informed and caring citizens ready to take their place as members of a participatory democracy. We want students who can lead moral, fulfilled lives *and* succeed in the workplace. We reject out of hand the suggestion that the purpose of schooling is to prepare students to be mere cogs in an economic machine. We believe strongly that a nation's economy should serve the needs of citizens, not the other way around. The value of individuals cannot be equated with their contributions to the economy.

Disproportionately high rates of poverty among Black, Hispanics and Native Americans is a strong indication that the current economic structures have failed utterly to serve the needs of many Americans and need to be rethought. The same argument can be made for the structures of schooling. The persistent, high level of academic failure among children living in poverty, Black and Hispanic students and English language learners is powerful evidence that something is seriously wrong with the structures of schooling. It is, therefore, imperative that we rethink the basic structures of school. In other words, we need to fix schools, not children – and this is not a matter of school choice. Teacher educators like me are committed to creating inclusive schools and classrooms that are considerate of the incredible range of ways our students live their lives. We reject competitive, one-size-fits-all schooling that devalues cultural and linguistic differences, where everyone is supposed to do better than everyone else, and that guarantees high levels of failure.

Recalling the question, "What is it about school that manages to transform children who are good at learning … into children who are not good at learning, if they are poor or members of certain minority groups?" (Gee, 2005, p. 10), I believe that the problem of academic underachievement among poor and minority groups lies in the pedagogy of poverty that focuses instruction on low-level skills to the exclusion of challenging curricula common in more affluent, high-achieving schools and classrooms. Many poor and minority children learn less because they are taught less, an argument I set forth earlier. Similar problems plague the schooling of English language learners and students with disabilities.

The neoliberal solution to the problem of high levels of academic failure among poor children and children who are members of minority groups is school choice. Presumably, if the market is left to work its magic in the form of vouchers and charter schools, poor schools will fail and a range of good schools will emerge to fulfill the needs of poor and minority students. Yet, the evidence indicates that, on average, charter schools do no better or worse than traditional public schools (Ravitch, 2013). Nor have the free-market inspired reforms embedded in the *No Child Left Behind Act* had much effect on the quality of schooling for poor and minority students. For example, NAEP data indicate that the achievement gap between children living in poverty and their more affluent peers has not diminished over the last decade (NAEP, 2013). Indeed, the NAEP achievement gap of 29 points in 4th grade reading in 2013 is slightly larger in magnitude than at any point since 2002, the first year NAEP data were disaggregated by economic groups and, coincidentally the year NCLB was signed into law.

Perhaps the biggest disappointment of neoliberal reforms to date has been the failure of such policies to affect the quality of curricular opportunities afforded to students in low-achieving schools. The "scientifically-based" reading practices mandated by *No Child Left Behind*, for example, have often been translated into a focus on low-level, basic skills (Gamse, Tepper-Jacob, Horst, Boulay & Unlu, 2008). Similarly, there is evidence indicating that charter schools, especially for-profit charters eager to minimize instructional costs, are adopting scripted, standardized reading curricula focused on low-level skills (Garcia, Barber & Molnar, 2009; Scott, 2009). Of course, prescriptive, standardized reading curricula can be taught by inexperienced, less qualified teachers who can be paid less, thereby maximizing profits, an instance of putting profits ahead of students.

We don't need to wait for market innovations to create better schools. Reading educators like me believe that excellent models of successful schools are readily available within traditional public schools serving affluent, high-achieving students, mainly in suburban school districts. As I described earlier, overall, US schools do an excellent job of educating children in low-poverty schools. We need to insure, however, that all students, whatever their background or assessed ability, have opportunities to engage with the same challenging curricula that is common in affluent schools. The pedagogy of poverty must be replaced by a pedagogy of affluence – the best, most engaging curriculum for everyone. This idea is fundamental to how reading educators like me think about the teaching of reading.

Teacher educators like me have a different sense of not only *how* to teach reading but also the *purpose* of reading instruction in our schools. In the context of market-based schooling, reading instruction is about learning the skills of reading that potential employers have deemed necessary for economic success. In this context reading is a commodity to be used in gaining employment. Certainly, we all want students to be prepared for the workplace and/or further education, but learning to read should not be limited to the mastery of a limited scope and sequence of finite skills. Reading educators like me aim to have students learn to engage with a range of texts for a variety of purposes, including finding pleasure in interacting with different kinds of texts. Learning to read should be about personal fulfillment as much as vocational skills and employment success.[18]

We also want students to learn to read critically – that is, citizens in a participatory democracy must to be able to consider how texts work to position and persuade readers to fulfill the author's intention. Reading critically means asking questions like:

- Who wrote this text and why?
- What do they want me to believe?
- How are groups of people portrayed – racial groups, women, people with disabilities?
- Whose views are excluded?
- Whose interests are served by this text?
- Is the information consistent with other sources?

Reading critically will help students learn to be informed consumers as well as informed citizens. Critical literacy also involves learning to use reading (and writing) for social action. Dozier, Johnston and Rogers (2006) put it this way:

> Critical literacy involves understanding the ways in which language and literacy are used to accomplish social ends. Becoming critically literate means developing a sense that literacy is for taking social action, an awareness of how people use literacy for their own ends, and a sense of urgency with respect to one's own literacy. (p. 18)

Increasingly, Twitter and other social media are being used effectively for social action, especially by young people. Reading educators like me aim to prepare all students to be able to use literacy to make a difference in the world. Making the world a better, more equal, and more just place is, for teacher educators like me, the ultimate goal of education.

Earlier, I lamented the fact that in our increasingly segregated schools and neighborhoods, there may be few opportunities to engage with people different from ourselves. The reading of literature, especially co-called multicultural literature, can be a way of learning more about how people different from ourselves live their lives. As Maxine Greene puts it, good literature has the power to allow our students to "… cross the empty spaces between ourselves and those we teachers have called 'other' over the years." (1995, p.3). Of course, contact with others, even in literature, can reinforce pernicious stereotypes (Britzman, 1991). Students will always need the guidance of thoughtful, skilled teachers to help them engage respectfully with the lives of others encountered in literature.

Finally, reading educators like me do not believe that pedagogical solutions to school failure will ever be sufficient for overcoming the debilitating effects of poverty that burden so many of our students. There are serious consequences of living in poverty, especially for children. Sue Books (2004) notes that

> Poor children bear the brunt of almost every imaginable social ill. In disproportionate numbers, they suffer hunger and homelessness; untreated sickness and chronic conditions such as asthma, ear infections, and tooth decay; lead poisoning and other forms of environmental pollution; and a sometimes debilitating level of stress created by crowded, run-down living spaces, family incomes that fall short of family needs, and ongoing threats of street violence and family dissolution. (p. 5)

Adverse experiences in early childhood, including poverty, have even been shown to have a lasting impact on children's developing brains, including the capacity to learn new skills and the ability to regulate stress (Shonkoff & Garner, 2012; Juster, McEwen & Lupien, 2010). The best reading methods, "scientifically-based" or not, will never be enough to overcome the material effects of poverty. If we, as a society, are truly committed to the rhetoric of *No Child Left Behind*, that ALL students succeed academically, we must commit ourselves to eliminating poverty. School choice can never eliminate poverty.

Regrettably, the neoliberal project that has taken hold of educational policy in this country is based on the conceit that only individuals control their fates, and if disproportionate numbers of poor children, Black students, Hispanic students, Native Americans and second language learners fail in school well, they need *choice*. If they still fail, as they most certainly will, then the fault is theirs.

Teacher educators like me firmly reject this cruel, mean-spirited vision of schools and society. Certainly, we want future teachers to be well prepared to teach reading, but we also want teachers who are kind and caring, and who are prepared to fight for social change. The free market cares little for children, so it is critically important that all of us, including teachers, do.

Notes

1. Following their discussion of these conclusions, Henry and Bastian suggest that higher admission standards and systematic data collection about graduates' performance, actions that NCTQ advocates, are directions for possible improvement in teacher education.

2. See Allington (2002) for a collection of critiques of the NRP report by a number of eminent reading researchers.

3. NCTQ used freedom of information laws to force compliance from most state universities.

4. The data for this analysis was based on a slight revision of the NCTQ evaluations of teacher preparation programs in December, 2013.

5. Note that although Black and Hispanic Americans are overrepresented among the poor, contrary to popular stereotypes, the largest group of poor Americans is White (US Census, 2013).

6. *Reading First* funds were made available to schools with the highest need in terms of reading proficiency and poverty status (Gamse et al., 2008).

7. See Dudley-Marling & Michaels (2012) for illustrations of high-expectation curricula in high poverty schools.

8. The NRP deliberately excluded from its review all research that failed to conform to its narrow vision of "scientifically-based" research and, in the process, excluded any research that didn't conform to its theoretical orientation to reading including ALL qualitative and correlational research. This could be seen to merely

be a methodological decision but, as I have attempted to show, methodological decisions always reflect theoretical orientation.

9. See Gruber & Vonèche (1977) for a comprehensive overview of Piaget's work.

10. See Brown, Goodman & Marek (1996) for a summary of miscue research.

11. For comprehensive reviews of the research base for meaning-based approaches to reading see Allington (2011); Braunger & Lewis (2006); and Kucer (2008) among others

12. See Rhodes & Dudley-Marling, 1996 as well as the report of the NRP.

13. During the 1991-1992 school year I took a leave from my academic duties to return to the classroom and teach 3rd grade.

14. See Dudley-Marling (1996) for a thorough discussion of explicit instruction within a whole language framework.

15. The NRP acknowledged a research base for invented spelling as a means of teaching phonics in its report.

16. See Goodman, Martens & Flurkey (2014) for an extended discussion of retrospective miscue analysis.

17. According to the National Alliance for Public Charter Schools, there are currently over 6,000 charter schools across 42 states and the District of Columbia, serving more than 2 million children. Sixty-seven percent of these charters are independently run "non-profit", single site schools; 20 percent are managed by "non-profit" organizations that run more than one charter school; and just under 13 percent are run by for-profit companies.

18. Interestingly, perhaps the biggest area of job growth is in the service sector where the literacy demands are typically quite low

References

Allington, R.L. (2002). (Ed.). *Big brother and the national reading curriculum: How ideology trumped evidence.* Portsmouth, NH: Heinemann.

Allington, R.L. (1983). The reading instruction provided readers of differing abilities. *The Elementary School Journal, 83(5),* 548-559.

Allington, R.L. (2000/2011). *What really matters for struggling readers: Designing research-based programs (3rd ed.).* New York: Longman.

Allington, R.L, Johnston, P.H. & Day, J.P. (2002). Exemplary fourth-grade teachers. *Language Arts, 79,* 462-466.

American Association of Colleges for Teacher Education (2015). *edTPA.* http://edtpa.aacte.org/state-policy

Anyon, J. (1980). Social class and the hidden curriculum of work. *Journal of Education, 162(1),* 67-92.

Babones, S. (May 9, 2015). Education "reforms" big lie: The real reason the right has declared war on our public schools. *Salon.* Accessed May 9, 2015 from http://www.salon.com/2015/05/09/education_reforms_big_lie_the_real_reason_the_right_has_declared_war_on_our_public_schools/

Berliner, D.C. (2013). Effects of inequality and poverty vs. teachers and schooling on America's youth. *Teachers College Record* Volume 115 (12) Date Accessed: 2/17/2015 http://www.tcrecord.org/library/abstract.asp?contentid=16889

Berliner, D.C. & Biddle, B.J. (1995). *The manufactured crisis: Myths, fraud and the attack on America's public schools.* New York: Basic Books.

Berliner, D. & Glass, G. (2014). *50 myths and lies that threaten America's public schools: The real crisis in education.* New York: Teachers College Press.

Bill & Melinda Gates Foundation (2015). *Awarded Grants.* Retrieved June 26, 2015 from http://www.gatesfoundation.org/How-We-Work/Quick-Links/Grants-Database#q/k=nctq:

Bishop, B. (2009). *The big sort: Why the clustering of like-minded Americans is tearing us apart.* Boston, MA: Mariner Books.

Books, S. (2004). *Poverty and schooling in the U.S.: Contexts and consequences.*

Erlbaum, Mahwah, NJ.

Braunger, J. & Lewis, J.P. (2006). *Building a knowledge base in reading (2nd ed.)*.Newark, DE: International Reading Association.

Britzman, D. (1991). Decentering discourses in teacher education: Or, the unleashing of unpopular things. *The Journal of Education, 173(3)*, 60-80.

Brown, J., Goodman, K., & Marek, A. (1996). *Studies in miscue analysis: An annotated bibliography*. Newark, DE: International Reading Association.

Buckley, S. (2012). Reading and writing for individuals with Down Syndrome – An overview. Retrieved from http://www.down-syndrome.org/information/reading/overview/

Bushism (n.d.). In *Wikipedia*. Retrieved on March 15, 2015 from http://en.wikipedia.org/wiki/Bushism

Chall, J.S. & Jacobs, V.A. (2003). Poor children's fourth-grade slump. *American Education, 27(1)*, 14-15, 44.

Chomsky N. (1959). Review of B. F. Skinner's *Verbal Behavior. Language, 35*, 26–58.

Chubb, J. E., & Moe, T. M. (1990). *Politics, Markets, and America's Schools*. Washington, DC: The Brookings Institution.

Cochran-Smith, M. (2014). Ed Reform and Teacher Education: Building Better Track or Trying to Stop the Train? *Keynote Address for the Annual Conference of the Teacher Education Division of the Council for Exceptional Children*. Indianapolis, Indiana: November 7, 2014.

Cochran-Smith, M. (2015). 'Ed Reform' and Teacher Education: The Policy Paradigm that is Reforming (Deforming?) Teacher Preparation in the U.S., *Teachers College Sachs Lecture Series*, Teachers College, Columbia, March 3, 2015.

Cochran-Smith, M. & Lytle, S. (2009). *Inquiry as stance: Practitioner research in the next generation*. New York: Teachers College Press.

Dozier, C., Johnston, P. & Rogers, R. (2006). *Critical literacy, critical teaching: Tools for preparing responsive teachers*. New York: Teachers College Press.

Dudley-Marling, C. (1996). Explicit instruction within a whole language framework. In E. McIntyre & M. Pressley (Eds.), *Balanced instruction: Strategies and skills in whole language* (pp. 23-38). Norwood, MA: Christopher Gordon.

Dudley-Marling, C. & Michaels, S. (Eds.) (2012). *High-expectation curricula: Helping all students succeed with powerful learning.* New York: Teachers College Press.

Dudley-Marling, C. & Paugh, P. (2004). *A classroom teacher's guide to struggling readers.* Portsmouth, NH: Heinemann.

Fairclough, N. (1989). *Language and power.* New York: Longman.

Finn, P.J. (2009). *Literacy with an attitude: Educating working-class children in their own self-interest.* Albany, NY: SUNY.

Friedman, M. (1955). The Role of Government in Education. In R.A. Solo (Ed.), *Economics and the Public Interest.* New Brunswick, NJ: Rutgers University Press.

Gallagher, K. (2009). *Readicide: How schools are killing reading and what you can do about it.* Portland, ME: Stenhouse.

Gamse, B.C., Tepper-Jacob, R., Horst, M., Boulay, B., & Unlu, F. (2008). *Reading First impact study: Final report.* Washington, DC: Institute for Education Sciences, U.S. Department of Education.

Garan, E.M. (2001). Beyond smoke and mirrors: A critique of the National Reading Panel report on phonics. *Phi Delta Kappan, 82,* 500-506.

Garcia, D.R., Barber, R. & Molnar, A. (2009). Profiting From Public Education: Education Management Organizations and Student Achievement. *Teachers College Record, 111(5),* 1352–1379.

Gee, J.P. (2004). *Situated language and learning: A critique of traditional schooling.* New York: Routledge.

Gee, J.P. (1990/2012). *Social linguistics and literacies: Ideology in discourses (4th ed.).* New York: Routledge.

Goodman, K. (1973). Miscues: "Windows on the reading process." In F. Gollasch (Ed.) *Language and literacy: The selected writings of Kenneth Goodman, Vol. I* (pp. 93–102). Boston: Routledge & Kegan Paul.

Goodman, Y.M., Martens, P. & Flurkey, A.D. (2014). The essential RMA – A window into readers' thinking. Katonah, NY: Richard C. Owen.

Greene, M. (1995). *Releasing the imagination: essays on education, the arts, and social change.* San Francisco, CA: Jossey-Bass.

Groff, P. (1996). Whole language: It's a matter of wrong assumptions. *Reading and Writing Quarterly: Overcoming learning difficulties, 12(2)*, 217-226.

Gruber, H. & Vonèche, J.J. (1977). *The essential Piaget.* New York: Basic Books.

Haberman, M. (1991). The pedagogy of poverty versus good teaching. *Phi Delta Kappan, 73*, 290-294.

Harvey, D. (2005). *A brief history of neoliberalism.* New York: Oxford University Press.

Hassard, J. (2013). What sort of teacher preparation programs does the Gates Foundation support. *The Art of Teaching Science*, November. http://www.artofteachingscience.org/what-sort-of-teacher-preparation-programs-does-the-gates-foundation-support/

Henry, K. & Bastian, K. (2015). Measuring Up: The National Council on Teacher Quality's Ratings of Teacher Preparation Programs and Measures of Teacher Performance. *The Education Policy Initiative at Carolina*, University of North Carolina.

Hess, F. & McShane, M. (Eds.) (2014). *Teacher Quality 2.0: Toward a New Era in Education Reform.* Cambridge, MA.: Harvard Education Press.

Hursh, D. W. (2007). Exacerbating inequality: The failed promise of the No Child Left Behind Act. *Race, Ethnicity and Education, 10(3)*, 295-308. (b)

Hursh, D. W. (2008). *High-stakes testing and the decline of teaching and learning: The real crisis in education.* New York: Rowman & Littlefield.

Jackson, A. (March 17, 2015). The Walmart family is teaching hedge funds how to profit from publicly funded schools. *Business Insider*. Accessed May 6, 2015 from http://www.businessinsider.com/walmart-is-helping-hedge-funds-make-money-off-of-charter-schools-2015-3

Juster, R.P., McEwen, B.S, & Lupien, S.J. (2010). Allostatic load biomarkers of chronic stress and impact on health and cognition. *Neuroscience and Biobehavioral Reviews, 35(1)*, 2-16.

Kliewer, C. (2008). *Seeing all kids as readers: A new vision for literacy in the inclusive early childhood classroom.* Baltimore, MD: Brookes.

Kozol, J. (2006). *The shame of the nation: The restoration of apartheid schooling in America.* New York: Broadway Books.

Krashen, S. (2001). More Smoke and Mirrors: A Critique of the National Reading Panel (NRP) Report on "Fluency." *Phi Delta Kappan, 83*, 119-123.

Krashen, S. (2013). Access to books and time to read versus the Common Core State Standards and tests. *English Journal, 103(2)*, 21–29.

Kucer, S.B. (2008). *What research really says about teaching and learning to read.* Urbana, IL: National Council of Teachers of English.

Kuhn, T. (1962). *The structure of scientific revolutions.* Chicago, IL: University of Chicago Press.

Lipman, P. (2007). "No child left behind:" Globalization, privatization, and the politics of inequality. In E. W. Ross & R. Gibson (Eds.), *Neoliberalism and education reform* (pp. 35-58). Cresskill, NJ: Hampton Press.

Martinez, E., & Garcia, A. (2000). *What is "neoliberalism?" A brief definition.* Retrieved October 30, 2010 from http://www.globalexchange.org/campaigns/econ101/neoliberalDefined.html

McDermott, R. (1976). *Kids make sense: An ethnographic account of the interactional management of success and failure in one first-grade classroom.* Ph.D. Dissertation, Stanford University.

McGuinn, P. (2012a). Fight Club: Are advocacy organizations changing the politics of education? *Education Next.* 12 (3).

McGuinn, P. (2012b). Stimulating Reform: Race to the top, Competitive Grants and the Obama Education Agenda, *Educational Policy, 26 (1)*: 136–159.

Manzo, K.K. (2006). After Complaint, Teacher Council Changes Rating. *Education Week, 25(42)*, 12.

Mock, D. & Kauffman, J. (2004). The delusion of full inclusion. In R.M. Foxx, J.W. Jacobson, & J.A. Mulick (Eds.), *Controversial therapies for developmental disabilities: Fad, fashion, and science in professional practice* (pp. 113-128). New York: Routledge.

Molnar, A. (Ed.). (2015). *Virtual schools in the U.S. 2015: Politics, performance, policy, and research evidence.* Boulder, CO: National Education Policy Center. Retrieved from http://nepc.colorado.edu/publication/virtual-schools-annual-2015

Murdoch, R. (October 15, 2011). The Steve Jobs model for educational reform. *The Wall Street Journal.* Accessed June 26, 2015 at http://www.wsj.

com/articles/SB10001424052970203914304576631100415237430

National Alliance for Charter Public Schools. *Get the facts.* Accessed October 23, 2014 from http://www.publiccharters.org/get-the-facts/

National Assessment of Educational Progress (NAEP) (2013). *The nation's report card.* Washington, DC: U.S. Department of Education, Institute of Education Sciences, National Center for Education Statistics. http://www.nationsreportcard.gov/ Data downloaded from: http://nces.ed.gov/nationsreportcard/naepdata/ and http://nces.ed.gov/nationsreportcard/naepdata/dataset.aspx

National Center for Children in Poverty (NCCP) (2014). *Demographics of poor children.* Accessed November 22, 2014 from www.nccp.org/profiles

National Center for Educational Statistics (NCES) (2014). Fast facts: International comparisons. Accessed February 18, 2015 from http://nces.ed.gov/fastfacts/display.asp?id=1

National Center for Educational Statistics (NCES) (2013). NAEP 2012: Trends in academic progress. Accessed June 26, 2015 from

http://nces.ed.gov/nationsreportcard/subject/publications/main2012/pdf/2013456.pdf

National Commission on Excellence in Education (1983). *A nation at risk: The imperative for educational reform.* Ann Arbor, MI: University of Michigan Press.

National Commission on Teaching and America's Future (2010). *Who will teach? Experience matters.* Washington, DC: Author.

National Council on Teacher Quality (2013). *Teacher Prep Review 2013 report* (June 2013, revised December 2013). Washington, DC.: Author. Retrieved from http://www.nctq.org/dmsStage/Teacher_Prep_Review_2013_Report

National Council on Teacher Quality (2014). *Teacher Prep Review 2014 report* (June 2014, revised February 2015). Washington, DC.: Author. Retrieved from http://www.nctq.org/teacherPrep/review2014.do

National Governors Association Center for Best Practices, Council of Chief State School Officers (2010). *Common Core State Standards (English Language Arts).* Washington, DC: Council of Chief State School Officers.

National Reading Panel. (1999). *Report of the National Reading Panel: Teaching children to read.* Washington, DC: Author.

Oakes, J. (2005). *Keeping track: How schools structure inequality (2nd ed.).* New Haven, CT: Yale University Press.

Paulson, E.J. & Freeman, A.E. (2003). *Insight from the eyes: The science of effective reading instruction.* Portsmouth, NH: Heinemann.

Payne, R.K. (2005). *A framework for understanding poverty (4th ed.).* Highlands, TX: Aha! Process, Inc.

Ravitch, D. (2010). *The death and the life of the great American school system: How testing and choice are undermining education.* New York: Basic Books.

Ravitch, D. (2013). *Reign of error: The hoax of the privatization movement and the danger to America's public schools.* New York: Knopf.

Ravitch, D. (June 18, 2013). That NCTQ report on teacher education: F. Retrieved from http://dianeravitch.net/2013/06/18/that-nctq-report-on-teacher-education-f/

Rhodes, L.K. & Dudley-Marling, C. (1996). *Readers and writers with a difference: A holistic approach to teaching struggling readers and writers.* Portsmouth, NH: Heinemann.

Rice, J.K. (2003). *Teacher quality: Understanding the effectiveness of teacher attributes.* Washington, DC: Economic Policy Institute.

Rosenblatt, L. M. (1994). *The reader, the text, the poem, the transactional theory of the literary work.* Carbondale, IL: Southern Illinois University Press.

Sawchuk, S. (October 8, 2013). For-profits dominate market for online teacher prep. *Education Week.* Accessed May 6, 2015 from http://www.edweek.org/ew/articles/2013/10/09/07online_ep.h33.html#

Scott, J.T. (2009) Managers of choice: Race, gender, and the philosophies of the new urban school leadership. In W. Feinberg & C. Lubienski (Eds.), *School choice policies and outcomes: Empirical and philosophical perspectives* (pp. 149-176). Albany, NY: State University of New York Press.

Shonkoff, J.P., & Garner, A.S. (2012). The lifelong effects of early childhood adversity and toxic stress. *Pediatrics, 129,* 1-17.

Simon, S. (August 2, 2012). Private firms eyeing profits from public schools. *Reuters.* Accessed May 5, 2015 at http://www.reuters.com/article/2012/08/02/us-usa-education investment-idUSBRE8710W220120802

Singer, A. (June 4, 2014). Why hedge funds love charter schools. *The Washington Post.* Accessed May 6, 2015 from http://www.washingtonpost.com/blogs/answer-sheet/wp/2014/06/04/why-hedge-funds-love-charter-schools/

Singer, A. (September 4, 2012). Pearson "Education" – Who are these people? *Huffington Post.* Accessed May 6, 2015 from http://www.huffingtonpost.com/alan-singer/pearson-education-new-york-testing-_b_1850169.html

Sirota, D. (August 15, 2013). School reformers give a lesson in corruption. *Salon.*(online). Accessed May 5, 2015 at http://www.salon.com/2013/08/15/school_reformers_give_a_lesson_in_corruption/

Smith, F. (1973). *Psycholinguistics and reading.* New York: Holt, Rinehart &Winston.

Smith, F. (1981). Demonstrations, Engagement and Sensitivity. *Language Arts, 58,*103-112.

Smith, F. (1979/2006). *Reading without nonsense* (4th ed.). New York: Teachers College Press.

Smith, F. (1988/2011). *Understanding reading: A psycholinguistic analysis of reading and learning to read* (6th ed.). New York: Routledge.

Snow, C.E., Burns, M.S & Griffin, P. (Eds). *Preventing reading difficulties in young children.* Washington, DC: National Academy Press.

US Census Bureau (2013). *Poverty.* Retrieved February 22, 2014 from http://www.census.gov/hhes/www/poverty/poverty.html

US Census Bureau (2015). New Census Bureau report analyzes U.S. population projections. March 20, 1015 from https://www.census.gov/newsroom/press-releases/2015/cb15-tps16.html

Walsh, K., Glaser, D., & Wilcox, D. D. (2006). *What education schools aren't teaching about reading and what elementary teachers aren't learning.* Washington, DC: National Council on Teacher Quality. Retrieved [date] from http://www.nctq.org/dmsView/What_Ed_Schools_Arent_Teaching_About_Reading_NCTQ_Report

Whitty, G., Power, S., & Halpin, D. (1998). *Devolution & choice in education: The school, the state and the market.* Melbourne, Australia: Australian Council for Educational Research.

Appendix

Table 1. State rankings on NCTQ criteria on first (2013) NCTQ/ *US News & World Report* evaluation of teacher education programs on early reading and average rankings of 2013 state NAEP scores for 4th grade reading

STATE	NCTQ 2013 Rank	NAEP 2013 ranking for 4th grade reading
Massachusetts	37	2
Maryland	6.5	2
New Hampshire	45.5	2
Connecticut	35.5	4
New Jersey	39	5.5
Virginia	19	5.5
Vermont	45.5	7
Florida	10.5	9
Minnesota	12	9
Colorado	8	9
Pennsylvania	27	12
Wyoming	45.5	12
Delaware	* N/A	12
Indiana	29	15
Washington	20.5	15
Maine	45.5	15
Kentucky	22.5	19
North Dakota	33	19
Ohio	14.5	19
Iowa	* N/A	19
New York	40.5	19
Kansas	45.5	24

Nebraska	22.5	24
Montana	33	24
Rhode Island	6.5	24
Utah	1	24
Missouri	14.5	28
North Carolina	17	28
Georgia	34	28
Wisconsin	25.5	30
Tennessee	40.5	31
Idaho	25.5	34
Oregon	45.5	34
Alabama	10.5	34
Illinois	24	34
Arkansas	20.5	34
South Dakota	45.5	37
Michigan	38	39
Oklahoma	5	39
Texas	13	39
Hawaii	17	41.5
West Virginia	9	41.5
Nevada	30	43.5
South Carolina	28	43.5
Arizona	33	45.5
California	17	45.5
Louisiana	3	47
Alaska	45.5	48.5
Mississippi	4	48.5
New Mexico	35.5	50.5
District of Columbia	2	50.5

* N/A – No programs reviewed in these states because data not made available

Table 2. Proportion of teacher education programs meeting NCTQ criteria by state on second (2014) NCTQ/*US News* & *World Report* evaluation of teacher education programs and 2013 state NAEP scores for 4th grade reading

STATE	Proportion of programs meeting NCTQ criteria in 2014 for early reading	NAEP 2013 score for 4th grade reading
Massachusetts	28%	232
Maryland	63%	232
New Hampshire	25%	232
Connecticut	11%	230
New Jersey	16%	229
Virginia	43%	229
Vermont	0%	228
Florida	54%	227
Minnesota	55%	227
Colorado	42%	227
Pennsylvania	34%	226
Wyoming	0%	226
Delaware	40%	226
Indiana	38%	225
Washington	30%	225
Maine	0%	225
Kentucky	23%	224
North Dakota	20%	224
Ohio	49%	224
Iowa	26%	224
New York	15%	224
Kansas	21%	223
Nebraska	36%	223

Montana	34%	223
Rhode Island	66%	223
Utah	72%	223
Missouri	35%	222
North Carolina	26%	222
Georgia	35%	222
Wisconsin	25%	221
Tennessee	19%	220
Idaho	34%	219
Oregon	0%	219
Alabama	36%	219
Illinois	26%	219
Arkansas	33%	219
South Dakota	20%	218
Michigan	32%	217
Oklahoma	79%	217
Texas	36%	217
Hawaii	40%	215
West Virginia	59%	215
Nevada	0%	214
South Carolina	20%	214
Arizona	28%	213
California	21%	213
Louisiana	100%	210
Alaska	50%	209
Mississippi	70%	209
New Mexico	13%	206
District of Columbia	66%	206

Table 3. Proportion of all children under 18 years of age living in poverty in 2013 by state and 2013 state NAEP scores for 4th grade reading

STATE	Proportion of all children living in poverty (*)	NAEP 2013 score for 4th grade reading
Massachusetts	15%	232
Maryland	13%	232
New Hampshire	11%	232
Connecticut	14%	230
New Jersey	14%	229
Virginia	15%	229
Vermont	14%	228
Florida	24%	227
Minnesota	14%	227
Colorado	17%	227
Pennsylvania	19%	226
Wyoming	16%	226
Delaware	17%	226
Indiana	22%	225
Washington	18%	225
Maine	19%	225
Kentucky	27%	224
North Dakota	12%	224
Ohio	23%	224
Iowa	16%	224
New York	22%	224
Kansas	18%	223
Nebraska	16%	223
Montana	19%	223
Rhode Island	20%	223
Utah	15%	223

Missouri	22%	222
North Carolina	25%	222
Georgia	25%	222
Wisconsin	18%	221
Tennessee	25%	220
Idaho	19%	219
Oregon	22%	219
Alabama	27%	219
Illinois	20%	219
Arkansas	26%	219
South Dakota	17%	218
Michigan	23%	217
Oklahoma	24%	217
Texas	25%	217
Hawaii	16%	215
West Virginia	24%	215
Nevada	22%	214
South Carolina	26%	214
Arizona	25%	213
California	23%	213
Louisiana	27%	210
Alaska	14%	209
Mississippi	32%	209
New Mexico	29%	206
District of Columbia	29%	206

National Center for Children in Poverty (2014), data for "all children living in poor families". "All children" includes children up to age 18 years.

About The Author Curt Dudley-Marling

Curt Dudley-Marling recently retired from Boston College after 33 years working in schools of education at universities in the US and Canada. Curt began his career as an elementary special education teacher working for 7 years in schools in Ohio and Wisconsin before earning his doctorate from the University of Wisconsin-Madison. Curt briefly resumed his classroom teaching career in the early 1990s, taking a one-year leave from his duties at York University in Toronto to teach 3rd grade.

Over the course of his academic career, Curt Dudley-Marling taught courses in language and literacy including early reading and writing methods courses for prospective teachers. He has published over 100 articles and book chapters and 14 books, much of this work focusing on language and literacy, Disability Studies, and classroom talk. Overall, his scholarship stands as a critique of deficit perspectives that implicate the families, culture, and language of students living in poverty in their high levels of school failure. His most recent research examines the effect of evidence-based discussion in elementary classrooms, particularly for students who are presumed to be at risk for educational failure.

In addition to his scholarly work, Curt has worked extensively in the schools helping teachers improve their practice with young readers and writers. Curt Dudley-Marling is a former co-editor of the NCTE journal Language Arts and former chair of NCTE's Elementary Section. In 2014 he was honored as the first Kate Welling Distinguished Scholar in Disability Studies at Miami University in Oxford, Ohio.

Other Books By Curt Dudley-Marling

Dudley-Marling, C. & Michaels, S. (Eds.) (2012). *High expectation curricula: Helping all students succeed with powerful learning.* New York: Teachers College Press. [U.K. Times Higher Education Suggested Reading List for 2013]

Dudley-Marling, C. & Gurn, A. (Eds.) (2010). *The myth of the normal curve.* New York: Peter Lang.

Dudley-Marling, C. & Paugh, P. (2009). *A classroom teacher's guide to struggling writers.* Portsmouth, NH: Heinemann.

Dudley-Marling, C. & Paugh, P. (2004). *A classroom teacher's guide to struggling readers.* Portsmouth, NH: Heinemann.

Dudley-Marling, C. (2000). *A family affair: When school troubles come home.* Portsmouth, NH: Heinemann.

Dudley-Marling, C. (1997). *Living with Uncertainty: The messy reality of classroom practice.* Portsmouth, NH: Heinemann.

Rhodes, L.K. & Dudley-Marling, C. (1996). *Readers and writers with a difference: A holistic approach to teaching struggling students, 2nd edition.* Portsmouth, NH: Heinemann Educational Books.

Made in the USA
Charleston, SC
15 December 2015